WARNER BROTHERS

Other Books by Charles Higham—

CECIL B. DEMILLE (1973)

ZIEGFELD (1972)

THE FILMS OF ORSON WELLES (1970)

HOLLYWOOD CAMERAMEN (1970)

THE CELLULOID MUSE: HOLLYWOOD DIRECTORS SPEAK (1970)

HOLLYWOOD IN THE FORTIES (1968)

WARNER
BROTHERS

CHARLES HIGHAM

CHARLES SCRIBNER'S SONS
New York

Copyright © 1975 Charles Higham

Library of Congress Cataloging in Publication Data

Higham, Charles
  The Warner Brothers.

  1. Warner Brothers Pictures, Inc.
PN1999.W3H5   791.43'0973   74-11019
ISBN 0-684-13949-9

1 3 5 7 9 11 13 15 17 19 V|C 20 18 16 14 12 10 8 6 4 2

Printed in the United States of America

For Richard Palafox

Author's Note

In preparing this history of the Warners studio, from its
foundation in 1918 to its decline in the 1950s, I have
been firmly guided by the clear memories of many people
as well as by contemporary press-sheets, production
notes, clippings and records. Peter Lev acted loyally as
my research assistant in the daunting task of compiling
data from the files, in many cases not indexed, of contemporary newspapers. I particularly valued the help of Bill
Schaefer, personal assistant to Jack Warner, who put me
in touch with many people I might not otherwise have
found; and of Helen Nigh Hickox, daughter of William
Nigh, who filled me in on details of the first Warner venture in New York, records of which have entirely van-
ished. Others who were wonderfully helpful in sharing
their memories with me were: Irene Rich, Minna Wallis,

Hal B. Wallis, Henry Blanke, Bette Davis, Joan Crawford, Robert Florey, Harold Grieve, Charles Van Enger, Marie Josephsen, Lyman Broening, Jane Duncan, Lee Garmes, William ("Buster") Collier, David Butler, Mrs. Lee De-Forest, George R. Groves, Mary Astor, Brynie Foy, Hal Mohr, Dolores Costello Barrymore, Robert Lord, May McAvoy, the late Winnie Lightner, Betty Compson, Howard Hawks, the late Edward G. Robinson, Joan Blondell, John Bright, Sheridan Gibney, Mervyn LeRoy, the late Lucien Hubbard, Lou Edelman, Busby Berkeley, Harry Warren, the late Jerry Wald, Mrs. Jerry Wald (Mrs. Prinzmetal), William Dieterle, Anton Grot (alive and well at 93), Seton I. Miller, Milton Krims, the late Ernest Haller, Mickey Rooney, the late Miriam Hopkins, the late Max Steiner, Patric Knowles, David Lewis, Sir Gerald Gardiner, Casey Robinson, Albert Maltz, John Howard Lawson, Cary Grant, Ted McCord, James Wong Howe, Irving Rapper, Catherine Turney, Gertrude Walker, Kent Smith, Kirk Douglas, Sid Hickox, Leigh Brackett, Delmer Daves, Alfred Hitchcock, King Vidor, Herbert Lightman, Curtis Bernhardt, Jean Negulesco, Virginia Kellogg, Gordon Douglas, Raoul Walsh, John Cromwell, Sid Luft, George Stevens, George Cukor, the late Judy Garland, Sid Hickox, James Mason, George Hopkins, and Gene Allen. Ann Bloch typed the book and was most helpful with suggestions.

Early
Struggles

Most Hollywood stu-
dios have been content simply to entertain; until 1954,
Warner Brothers also sought to instruct. Its films are the
least dated and the most concerned with serious themes.
Its dialogue, beginning with the first talking films, was
very often on a high level of intelligence. Its stars, Bette
Davis, James Cagney, Humphrey Bogart and the rest, laid
down the naturalistic rules of screen talkie acting in the
1930s. Warners was a studio which rejected the schmaltz
so beloved of the other studios, particularly M-G-M. It
was cynical, alert, committed, sharp-witted. It dealt una-
bashedly in lowlife. It showed American greed and ac-
quisitiveness with a Dreiserian honesty. Jack Warner
always tried to give the impression of being a buffoon; in
fact, he was perhaps the ablest administrator in the his-

tory of Hollywood, with the showman's knack of surrounding himself with the best people available.

Not that Jack Warner, or his brothers, had the characteristics of latter-day saints. They would not have made millions by dispensing noble uplift to their employees. They were remorseless. They were ambitious beyond belief. They stood for no slacking. They drove their people like slaves. Their humor was cold and pitiless.

Yet despite everything, they were important men of our time. Their studio was as powerful as a major newspaper, dealing vigorously with crooked politics, with the Mafia, with the prohibition gangs, with the lack of privileges of women in a male-dominated society, with the ugliness of theatrical life. Even their musicals were unlike any others: bitter and acrid portraits of the realities of show business. They exposed the evils of newspaper reporting. By their pioneering efforts they attacked racial prejudice in the Deep South and had the chains struck from the ankles of the prison gangs in Georgia. They provided biographies of heroes of science and literature.

In the war years, they acted vigorously as an organ of propaganda for Roosevelt. After the war, they returned to their pioneering stance and exposed conditions in women's prisons and (again) in the Deep South. Their last great films, A Star Is Born and the James Dean trilogy, summed up all of their social comment and incomparable technical command, before two of the brothers sold out and the studio lost its individual character.

The brothers had widely differing personalities. Harry was cold, hard, and driving. But he was a great patriot, with a passionate love of America. Jack was, on the surface—and is today—a brittle would-be vaudeville clown, emitting a constant flow of bad jokes, as though performing at a lifelong party. Bronzed and natty, suited by the finest tailors, he is reminiscent of Errol Flynn and John Barrymore—his friends and idols. At 82, he is as facetious and as tough as ever. He is a very hard man. But underneath the front of callous humor, he is to this day a passionately committed picture-maker. Albert and Sam were mild and pleasant, the latter an urgent pursuer of the best in film-making until his tragically early death on the eve of the first performance of *The Jazz Singer* in 1927. Sam had a touch of genius, not quite shared by Jack. The sisters were largely colorless women, who have no part in the story. David suffered tragically from encephalitis from his youth, until his death in 1939, and Milton died while still at college.

The Warner parents, Benjamin and Pearl, were both born in Poland in 1857. Much of their lives was spent in the muddy, depressing little village of Krasnashiltz, near the Russian border. Benjamin was a cobbler, whose days were an insufferable ordeal of poverty and physical discomfort.

In 1881, the couple's eldest son, Harry Morris, was born, and Sam in 1888. Benjamin migrated on a cattle boat to New York. He went to Baltimore, Maryland, because a friend had preceded him there. He took lodgings in the Skid Row district, and set up a cobbler's shop on the intersection of Pratt and Light Streets. In 1895 the rest of the family followed—Pearl, Harry, and a little girl, Anna. A new son, Albert, was born. The cobbler's business proved slow, and on an impulse Benjamin Warner left the shop in his wife's charge and traveled around selling pots and pans. While on his travels, he heard that money was to be made in Canada from trading kitchenware for furs. For two years he traveled across Canada, trying to scrape a living, with his family stuffed into a wretched wagon behind him. In London, Ontario, during a brief pause in this unhappy journey, Jack Warner was born in 1892.

In 1893, the family, defeated by the cold of Canada, arrived in Youngstown, Ohio, where another son, David, was born.

When the family arrived in Youngstown, it was in a state of violent unrest. It was a dark, depressing and chaotic city: the mayor shared the tasks of police, judge and executive, the city council was unpaid, the police force was more suitable for a small town than a city of 35,000 people. In the early 1890s, the situation was beginning to improve, but the changes were achieved with anguish. In the spring of 1893, shortly after the family settled in, a strike completely paralyzed the city. The steel mills closed down. Business failed, and the financial structure of the city gave way.

Even established Youngstown families suffered from poverty, and it has been estimated that in 1893 and 1894, many families had no income at all. Depressed, angry, and hungry men and women milled through the streets with nothing to do. The lines at the soup kitchens were long. There were hundreds of beggars everywhere. Life was cheerless and desperate.

For the Warners, it was almost as dreadful an existence as theirs had been in Poland. Few people could afford shoe repairs, no matter how low Benjamin depressed the prices. The various hovels the family lived in had no plumbing to speak of, and a "shower" was a trip to the pump in the yard. Yet Mrs. Warner was a wonderful cook, managed to make ends meet, and even entertained many starving people with Kosher cooking in her mean and tiny kitchen. The boys, in spite of everything, were able to obtain their strength and robustness playing baseball and football. All of the boys except Jack, who was never scholarly, went finally to Rayen High School.

A new daughter, Sadie, was born in 1895, and Milton, who later died of peritonitis, in 1896. Other children died in infancy. With the appalling diet, cramped living conditions and lack of ventilation, only the toughest could survive with health intact. And Harry, Albert and Jack were certainly tough.

4

Early Struggles

In 1900, Albert Warner set out for Chicago to find work. He joined the Swift organization as a trainee salesman. He was taught how to sell soap. He was given a suitcase and a territory to sell it in. After two weeks he was proven to be a failure. At first he thought he would return to Youngstown and try to work in the steel mills which had now resumed production, but he remembered his mother had warned him that was very dangerous work.

He screwed himself up to the task of selling soap successfully. One night he lined up all the different varieties of soap he had to sell on the bureau of his cheap Chicago lodging house room and walked up and down in front of them practicing his sales pitch for the next day. He even carried a cake in his pocket which he would take out and hold as he spoke to a prospect. But despite all these elaborate rehearsals, his efforts were useless.

Then he hit on a marvelous idea. He would give away one box of soap for every box bought. The plan succeeded, and Albert made a great success for the company in both Illinois and Pennsylvania.

While in Pittsburgh in 1904, Harry Warner saw his first motion picture. Harry Davis had opened his first nickelodeon on Pittsfield Street, showing two features a week, with a program change on Mondays and Thursdays. Harry, a solid, cool, driving 23-year-old, had no interest in a new art form. But when he saw people standing in line in the rain to see the flickering images of love and violent action he suddenly realized this might be a good new business to investigate. He resigned his job at once and left for Youngstown to discuss the matter with his brothers.

One of the brothers, Sam, shared his enthusiasm. Sam had already fallen in love with movies: he loved their dash, their excitement. He had operated the first projection machine movement used in a Youngstown nickelodeon. He had even persuaded his father to pawn a watch

5

and chain to buy the projector when the owner went broke. Sam was now the proud owner of one of the few projectors in Youngstown. He also had a copy of *The Great Train Robbery.* He and Harry wrote to the managers of opera houses in various surrounding towns, offering to provide "moving picture shows" between the acts of traveling companies. A few bothered to answer. It was a start. Setting out by trolley, the family with the print of *The Great Train Robbery* began their little entertainments. Sam cranked the projector; Rose, age 13, played piano; Jack, already a bright, snappy nascent comedian, sang the illustrated songs from the slides and performed in blackface. When the film broke, which was often, Sam would flash on a slide conveniently reading "Two minute intermission."

Back in Youngstown at the end of the tour, Harry tried to secure a permanent theatre for the show. It was impossible. Store owners refused to allow conversions to theatres. Finally after writing to some 50 towns and cities, he awakened the interest of a storekeeper in Newcastle, Pennsylvania, who allowed him to convert his building. There was no money for chairs. The brothers borrowed them from an undertaker on the proviso that if anyone died and a funeral took place, the chairs would be returned at once.

The motion picture business was, even in those early boom days, a very precarious one. Quite often, important films were not delivered. Prints had to be run from one theatre to another in the same day. Harry decided by degrees that no single exhibitor could operate alone. He contacted a number of equally hard-up theatre owners and formed a joint exchange for the wide showing of motion pictures—this became known as the Duquesne Amusement Supply Company, the first of such organizations in America. Its headquarters was in Pittsburgh, and it prospered rapidly. But the producers of the films themselves gradually became aware that the exchange company was profiting at their expense, and they deliberately supplied them with second-rate films and prints, raised the rentals to astronomical heights, and refused to supply short features at all. After a hopeless struggle, Harry Warner gave in and sold the entire outfit to the General Film Company.

During that period, the brothers were constantly shifting their base of operations. In St. Louis, they made two-reel Westerns called *Peril of the Plains* and *Raiders of the Mexican Border*, which Sam directed. In 1912, Sam went to Los Angeles to set up a film exchange, while Jack went to San Francisco to set up another. There he met a pretty blonde girl called Irma and married her. The brothers began to distribute films instead of making them, netting large sums from such films as *War Brides*, with Nazimova. An early studio was set up at Santa Paula, California. Meanwhile the Warner parents moved into a large and comfortable white frame house in Youngstown. But the brothers' entire fortune was lost when they released *The Crisis*, made by the Selig Polyscope Company. An historical film about the Civil War, it was entirely inappropriate for audiences in 1917, when America entered World War I, and it cost the brothers $100,000.

The turning point in their fortunes came later in 1917. Sam and Jack Warner were in Los Angeles desultorily making slapstick comedies in a shabby little studio when they noticed an advertisement in a shop window for a forthcoming serialization in the *Los Angeles Examiner* of Ambassador James W. Gerard's famous book, *My Four Years in Germany*. They immediately cabled Gerard in Washington offering him a substantial sum for the rights and pretending they had a studio to film the story in.

Harry Warner traveled to Washington to see Gerard, and told him that he would make a strictly fair business arrangement. He would have to make the film on a share-of-profits contract, because the Warners had no capital. Gerard was sufficiently impressed by Harry Warner's enthusiasm to accept the arrangement, even though he had a more substantial offer from Famous Players-Lasky. He would receive one-fourth of the profits.

My Four Years in Germany was little more than a loosely strung together narrative. But its violent propagandist stance, calling for bloody vengeance against the Hun, was ideally suited to the temper of a country newly at war. It was ably directed by a new man, hitherto only known for Keystone comedies and social dramas, William Nigh, who prepared the script with Gerard himself and with Charles A. Logue.

Nigh was tall and slender, highly sensitive and passionately dedicated to the art of film. With his wife, Elizabeth, and his adopted daughter, Helen, he lived in a first floor brownstone apartment on 49th Street near Broadway. The well-known actress Nora White lived on the floor above. Nigh used to be driven by his Irish chauffeur John to the Biograph Studios at dawn in his very distinctive Mercedes with a Victoria top and brass headlights. It was a showpiece in New York. Sometimes his wife and daughter would come by subway and watch the shooting. At night, after an exhausting day, they would all go dancing after supper, or have the Warners and that great friend of the family, Richard Travers, come to dinner, or drop over to Jack Warner's apartment on Riverside Drive. Sometimes Nigh would have his great friend Rudolph Friml over for musicales, or drop down to Harlem to see jazz. At times during the shooting Helen Nigh would walk Jack and Irma Warner's baby, Jack Jr., in his carriage alongside the river.

Many scenes of *My Four Years in Germany* were shot in northern New York State, which effectively stood in for Germany itself. In the studio, which consisted mostly of one large stage under a high roof, Nigh marvelously designed and executed impressionist sets of the Kaiser's court, of various chancelleries and embassies and meeting places, all on the most slender budget. The uniforms and costumes were cadged from various New York companies at minimum rentals.

The film was beautifully photographed by Jack Sullivan, and the make up, supervised by Nigh and Sullivan themselves, was very skillful. The cast of hundreds was drawn from the very rich range of Broadway players available at the time.

Although William Nigh clashed constantly with Harry and Jack, and felt that they were incapable of either producing or exploiting the picture, when everything was over they all rejoiced in the results. Vibrant, passionate, based on Griffithian principles of editing, the film was a directorial triumph, and assured Nigh a long and successful career in the movies.*

My Four Years in Germany opened at the Knickerbocker Theatre in New York in March, 1918, to a tremendous public response. *The Moving Picture World* reported on the occasion in its issue of March 23:

"The screen version of Ambassador James W. Gerard's book, *My Four Years in Germany*, opened at the Knickerbocker Theatre, Sunday evening, March 10, to a body of spectators that filled every seat in the house and showed its appreciation of the picture by frequent outbursts of applause and also by hearty cheers when a particularly strong appeal was made to its patriotism. *My Four Years in Germany* is not a photoplay, but a historical document that sets forth in clear and concise terms the facts that led to the United States' entrance into the Great War.

"The Kaiser and his war lords are introduced, Ambassador Gerard being the central figure. The subject is han-

---

* Still dissatisfied with the Warners, Nigh left them in the 1920s and went to work for Louis B. Mayer.

dled in a dignified manner, but Germany's double-dealing and inhuman methods in her desire for conquests are shown in their true light.

"Charles A. Logue, who made the scenario, displays excellent judgment in his choice of material. There are scenes of blood and horror, but they are never overdone, and America's reply to the Kaiser's remark that the United States wouldn't fight is worked up into a stirring patriotic finish as the troops of the Allies and then the soldiers of Uncle Sam are shown marching eagerly to the defense of justice and humanity."

Ambassador Gerard occupied a box at the opening and, when the last reel had been run off, there were loud calls for a speech. The spectators were on their feet, but resumed their seats when the Ambassador began his remarks. After referring to the screen's ability to bring home the facts concerning Germany's crimes against civilization, Mr. Gerard voiced his hearty approval of the picture and his faith in its success as an important aid in educating the people.

My Four Years in Germany, which may be said to have been the first war propaganda film made in the United States, made one million dollars gross profits and firmly launched the Warner brothers. They had been struggling along in various studios in different parts of Los Angeles—most recently in a dilapidated structure in Culver City. Quite clearly, the time had come to make a move, and they settled on a property in Hollywood.

The land had originally been developed by William Beesemyer, a son of German immigrants, who had bought some property in the Cahuenga Valley—later known as Hollywood *—in 1874. He built a ranch house and barns

---

* They were also offered 342 acres on Pico Boulevard by a man called Harry Janss. Since it was so far out, the area was thought to be unsuitable for picture-making and the brothers turned it down. Janss offered them the land free of charge in return for their put-

on 160 acres which later included a stretch of Sunset Boulevard. The area that the Warners finally bought consisted of only 10 acres, on the extreme eastern end of the property, near Bronson and Sunset. The charming and gracious Beesemyer family agreed to a price of only $25,000, with no deposit and $1500 a month. There the brothers built for a quarter of a million dollars a rambling structure with a line of imposing white columns in the front which they called their studio. The dressing rooms and the offices were shabby, the $50,000 sound stage roughly carpentered.

The brothers' staff grew by degrees, including Hal Wallis, a young publicity man, and his sister, Minna, a secretary.

From the very outset, the brothers began their policy of making frank and outspoken films dealing with important social themes. In 1919, the brothers made their next important feature, *Open Your Eyes*, shot under the careful supervision of the Public Health Service. Semi-documentary in approach, it explored the subject of syphilis, again some 20 years before the first, supposedly "revolutionary" Warner treatment of the subject in *Dr. Ehrlich's Magic Bullet*. Jack Warner played a young soldier. *Open Your Eyes*, directed by Gilbert P. Hamilton and starring Claire Binney as a woman stricken with a "social disease," was amply illustrated with shots of the final stages of the disease, charts, and a scrupulously researched historical background, designed as a caution to departing doughboys.

Alongside these contributions to politics and the study of medicine, the brothers began to make a series of amusing comedies, more or less in the Mack Sennett mold, with Al ("Fuzzy") St. John, a member of the Keystone

---

ting up a sound stage. Profits would then be shared. They refused, and William Fox accepted the arrangement. The land turned out to be Century City, worth scores of millions today.

Cops who went on to make hundreds of movies. Simultaneously, the brothers began to assume the individual roles they were to occupy for the rest of their lives. Harry Warner was chiefly situated after the early 1920s in New York, where he ran the theatre end of the business, the gradually increasing chains of theatres into which the studio's products automatically flowed. Albert became the treasurer, in theory controlling the family's financial affairs, though in fact in many ways his role was only nominal. He exerted little influence on policy after the earliest period. Jack and Sam were more and more frequently in Hollywood; Jack gradually assumed the complete control of all production on the West Coast, hiding his immense shrewdness and grasp of public taste behind a clown's mask.

In 1921, the Warners moved into a series of dramas dealing with pressing social themes. *Ashamed of Parents*, directed by Horace G. Plympton, was rather startlingly autobiographical. Silas Wadsworth is obviously based on Benjamin Warner: a shoemaker who struggled to send his son Arthur (clearly, this was Milton Warner) to college. He is pleased to see him become a football star. The social background, both of the college and of the family life, was carefully and affectionately evoked. *Parted Curtains*, directed by James C. Bradford and John Bracken (who took over when Bradford fell ill), has the distinction of being the first Warner film to deal with the theme of crime. Joe Jenkins, played by Henry B. Walthall, is released from jail, and, after a futile search for work, tries to steal some money from a painter, Wheeler Masters (Edward Cecil). Masters sets about to reform the would-be thief. It was a theme which would crop up in many situations in Warner films for 30 years. *School Days* was directed and written by Nigh, and photographed by Sid Hickox, who in later years shot such famous Warner films as *To Have and Have Not* and *The Big Sleep*. It was based on a famous Gus Edwards song. The story was again to do with reform: it was the account of a young boy raised very strictly and austerely, who is treated disdainfully when he enters the high society of New York. He becomes involved with a criminal gang and returns, embittered but spiritually purged, to his small town. The entire story turned up in the Warner film *Big City Blues* more than a decade afterward. Although Paramount announced four years later that *Underworld*, directed by Joseph Von Sternberg, was the first gangster film, the brothers made what was almost certainly the first in this story of the dark life of the Big City. *Why Girls Leave Home*, also directed by Nigh, with Anna Q. Nilsson in the leading role, was again the story of a simple person shocked by the corruption of "high life." These films not only reflected the brothers' parvenu background and suspicion of those who inherited wealth, they appealed strongly to the vast masses of the underprivileged at the outset of the 1920s, and had a strong, somewhat risqué contemporary flavor.

Production was still very slow at the studio. Fortunately, however, the brothers' parlous financial situation was alleviated by a financier, Motley Flint, who was a director of the Security Bank of Los Angeles. Solid, generous, thoughtful, Flint proved a fine mainstay. His introduction to Jack Warner by their mutual masseur, Abdul, proved to be of inestimable benefit in the period leading up to the Wall Street crash. He made the brothers a series of loans which virtually kept them afloat until their comedies, social dramas, serials and action films began to earn a sufficient profit.

In 1922, the film-making policy continued at about five films a year. *Heroes of the Street* was another gangster/action feature presaging the studio's policy some years later. William Beaudine directed the picture from a screenplay by the accomplished British writer (and later director) Edmund Goulding, and Mildred Considine.

Eddie DuPar, who was to be the prime mover in photographing the first talkies, was the cameraman. A policeman is killed and a gang leader, known as the Shadow, is suspected. The policeman's son, aided by a courageous chorus girl, again an early example of a Warner type—smart, wisecracking, enterprising in the flushing out of crime—sets out to disclose the truth. *Rags to Riches*, directed by Wallace Worsley, from a story by Nigh and Walter de Leon, is in the same category. The freckled, fresh-faced Wesley Barry, popular at the time, plays Marmaduke Clarke, a playboy who joins a gang. Attempts are made to kidnap him, and he runs into criticism from local bluenoses, before he cleanses his reputation and wins the girl. As in all of these early Warner films, the milieu is simple, either low-class urban or rural. Here, too, the basis for the whole Warner approach to environment was laid down.

In 1920, Jack and Sam Warner co-directed an exciting 15-episode serial, also released as a seven-reel feature, *A Dangerous Adventure*. It was designed to cash in on the current vogue of films featuring animal stars. The co-directors used an entire travelling circus—the Al G. Barnes troupe and animals—for the film. The story was exciting: two sisters, Marjorie and Edith Stanton, played by Grace Darmond and Derelys Perdue, are seeking a hidden treasure in Central Africa. They are kidnapped by a jungle chief, and are rescued by two brave young men. An elephant ran amuck, a leopard mauled an assistant to death, a monkey attacked Jack Warner, and the two stars quarreled constantly. The direction was clumsy, and the film did not recoup its costs until it was released as a seven-reel feature in 1922, but it was an enthralling diversion.

2

Ambitious
Ventures

Throughout the early 1920s, Motley Flint's encouragement permitted the brothers to enjoy a period of rapid expansion, to effect the purchase of many important properties, and to achieve a series of improvements of the studio at Sunset and Bronson. In December, 1922, and January, 1923, they invested $250,000 in the effective rebuilding and enlarging of the offices and sound stages. A gifted, if crude and ill-tempered administrator, Harry Rapf (later to have a successful career at Metro-Goldwyn-Mayer) joined the executive staff as a production chief, and David Belasco, the magnifico of the Broadway stage, accepted, after eight years of refusing other companies, a contract with the Warners to supervise film versions of his productions *The Gold-Diggers*, *Deburau*, and *Daddies*. He received $250,000 for the rights to these three plays, in addition to a percentage of the profits of each production. He agreed to edit the scripts and to cooperate in the preparation of the continuity. He offered the original costumes from his wardrobes, and many members of the original casts. *The Los Angeles Times* announced in an article dated January 24, 1923: "The effect of Mr. Belasco's allying himself with the silent drama will be profound among producers of motion pictures. The magic of 'David Belasco presents' flickering in a motion picture title is expected to pave the way to greater and better things in the industry."

In February, Jack Warner held a press conference to declare publicly that a large library was being established at Sunset and Bronson, containing volumes on photography "of every description," books on building for the technical department, and "fiction aplenty." In New York, Sam Warner arranged for the librarian of New York University, Melvin Hudgins, to come out as custodian of the great collection. Jack Warner said: "In my opinion this library will prove a godsend to the actors and actresses who have to wait around the studio until the director is ready for them. It will also be very helpful to us in selecting stories for our future 'classics of the screen,' as there will be hundreds of books in it which we can read and possibly use."

In March, 1923, a new interior stage was completed, with dressing rooms and scenery storage rooms alongside it. The stage was 370 feet by 140 feet, thus occupying more than 64,000 square feet of space, where six companies could work at once. It was designed by Lewis Gleb, technical director for Warners, and Enas Hartley, the brothers' chief construction engineer. A new electrical plant, with F. N. Murphy as chief electrical engineer, was also installed.

In New York, David Belasco gave his views on his future association with Warners: "There are great thoughts which can only be expressed by silence, so said St. Martin a long time ago. It was this thought in its relation to a new way of telling a story that lured me into moving pictures. The motion picture has come to stay. It has possibilities of amazing delicacy and they have come into a consciousness of its purpose."

Along with the widely publicized arrangements for Belasco, the brothers instituted a series of high society dramas starring Irene Rich, and a policy of buying literary works of quality: Olga Printzlau adapted Scott Fitzgerald's *The Beautiful and Damned,* directed by William A. Seiter, with Marie Prevost and Kenneth Harlan; Julien Josephson adapted *Main Street,* Sinclair Lewis' novel of Gopher Prairie, directed by Harry Beaumont with Florence Vidor as Carol Milford and Monte Blue as Dr. Will Kennicott; Olga Printzlau was the adapter again of Edith Wharton's *The Age of Innocence,* with Edith Roberts as Countess Ellen Olenska and Elliot Dexter as Newland Archer, admirably directed by Wesley Ruggles; and Dorothy Farnum adapted *Babbitt,* directed by Harry Beaumont, with Willard Louis as George F. Babbitt, and Carmel Myers as Tanis Judique. Other Warner films of distinction were *Brass,* from Charles Gilman Norris' *Brass: a Novel of Marriage,* about life on a California fruit ranch, ably directed by Sidney Franklin and written by Julien Josephson; *Little Johnny Jones,* based on George M. Cohan's famous play, directed by Arthur Rosson (later DeMille's assistant director) and Johnny Hines; Kathleen Norris' *Lucretia Lombard,* with Irene Rich excellent in the title role, directed by Jack Conway and adapted by Bertram Millhauser and Sada Cowan; Belasco's production of his own stage presentation *Tiger Rose,* with his mistress Lenore Ulric repeating her stage performance under the direction of Sidney Franklin; and Ernest Pascal's *The Dark Swan,* adapted by Frederick Jackson and directed by Millard Webb, with Marie Prevost and Monte Blue.

From the character of all of these ventures, it can be seen that the Warners were not satisfied with their primary role as makers of the action film. They were conscious, as outsiders and upstarts in Hollywood, of the need to prove that they could encourage "art" as well. If theirs was to be a great studio, commanding respect and awe from its competitors, they must obtain rights to superior fiction, and engage at least one director of international reputation. For a time, they considered hiring Cecil B. DeMille, who in 1923 had grown disaffected with Adolph Zukor, his employer at Famous Players-Lasky, for what he felt to be interferences with his production of *The Ten Commandments.* But they finally decided—and Motley Flint confirmed them in their decision—that De-Mille was far too extravagant and demanding for their particular plans. They settled instead on Ernst Lubitsch, the most prominent director in Europe.

Lubitsch had a mixed ancestry, including Polish and Hungarian elements. He was the son of a tailor, born in Berlin on January 28, 1892. His education at the Sophien-Gymnasium had been sketchy, and he was impatient with school, leaving it at 16, despite his father's grave objections, to take up the life of a theatrical performer. Working as an extremely inefficient bookkeeper in his father's shop by day, he played, with the encouragement of the actor Victor Arnold, as a knockabout comic in music halls at night. Devoid of looks or fine physique, he was unable to obtain serious acting roles. Nevertheless, by his late teens he had developed a remarkable personality. Electric, dynamic, he cracked with wit and intelligence. Not handsome, but fascinating, he had jet-black, twinkling eyes, straight black hair slicked down with oil and parted on the right, an impish high-cheekboned face and a small, stocky

body, the movements of which were alive with humor.
Even as an adolescent he chain-smoked cheap cigars incessantly, and had a habit of pacing up and down while
talking, his hands clasped behind his back and his stomach protruding Napoleonically.

Max Reinhardt, with his unfailing eye for talent,
engaged Lubitsch for his Deutsches Theatre on the Schumannstrasse in Berlin in 1911. The young man distinguished himself—after a series of supporting roles—as the
hunchback in *Sumurun*, starring Leopoldine Konstantin.
A year later, in 1912, Lubitsch was working not only in
the Deutsches Theatre but in his spare time at the Bioskop Film Studio as an assistant property man. He began
working in 1913 as a comedian in film productions: one of
these, *Die Firma Heiratet,* was based on an autobiographical story of his own, suggested by his own
ineptitude in his father's shop. The film and its successor,
Die Stolz Der Ferma, were very successful, and as a result, Lubitsch during World War I began writing, directing and appearing in his own crude comedies. He also appeared with great success at the Apollo Theatre as a
burlesque clown. A considerable advance in his career
took place when he began working with the young Pola
Negri in *Vendetta* and *Die Augor der Mummie Ma* (*The
Eyes of the Mummy Ma*), and when he began an important collaboration with the writer Hans Kräly in *Ich
Mochte Kawin Mann Sein* (*I Don't Want to Be a Man*).

Kräly was destined to be Lubitsch's right-hand man.
Tall, commanding, and crop-haired, with the build and
bearing of a Prussian officer, he had the education, the
grand bourgeois social background Lubitsch entirely
lacked. He guided him into the fringes of that Berlin
world of the *haut ton* to which Lubitsch's lower-class
Jewish origins forbade access. Through Kräly, Lubitsch
learned the art of sophisticated comedy which was to become his trademark. He also learned the art of Ferenc

Molnár, the great Hungarian playwright to whom Kräly was utterly devoted, and who deeply influenced Kräly's work, and subsequently Lubitsch's own.

In 1919, Lubitsch and Kräly together created the comedy *Die Austernprinzessin* (*The Oyster Princess*), which was in essence a forerunner of their great comedies later on. It was the story of an heiress to an oyster fortune, who with her father tries to crash into Prussian high society. Like so many of Lubitsch's films, it contained an autobiographical streak: his own largely ill-judged attempt to become part of Berlin society was effectively commented upon in the action. Lubitsch and Kräly again collaborated on the brilliantly stylized *Madame DuBarry*, a film as diverting today as when it was made. It was a marvel of sophistication, astonishing—in view of Lubitsch's parvenu background—as a portrait of the court of Louis XV, played to perfection by Pola Negri as Mme DuBarry, by Emil Jannings as the corrupt Louis XV, and above all by Reinhold Schunzel, a model of adroit wickedness, as the Duc de Choiseul. The film displayed to a fault Lubitsch's elegant and feline directorial precision: each gesture, each tiny detail of physical movement was choreographed with an extraordinary intelligence.

The subsequent triumphs of *Die Püppe* (*The Doll*), with Ossi Oswalda, *Sumurun*, in which Lubitsch recreated for the screen his original role of the hunchback; *Anna Boleyn*, with Henny Porten as Anne Boleyn and Jannings as Henry VIII, and *Das Weib des Pharo* (*The Wife of Pharoah*), firmly established Lubitsch as a nonpareil in his field. Inevitably, he was invited to Hollywood. When he received a telegram at EFA Studios in Berlin from Douglas Fairbanks and Mary Pickford asking him if he would direct *Dorothy Vernon of Haddon Hall*, he left for America at once, with his young and amusing assistant Heinz (Henry) Blanke, on the *S. S. Republic*, and stayed at the Ambassador Hotel in New York, before leaving for Hollywood on the Santa Fe Limited. On the journey across the Atlantic, both Lubitsch and Blanke decided they did not like *Dorothy Vernon of Haddon Hall;* that it was unmitigated sentimental nonsense and a waste of their time.

They were met off the train at the old Santa Fé Railroad Depot in Los Angeles by the young French assistant director, Robert Florey, who drove them to United Artists in a studio limousine. After many weeks of consideration, they decided firmly not to make *Dorothy Vernon of Haddon Hall.* Another projected idea, a version of *Faust,* with Miss Pickford as Marguerite, was rejected when Miss Pickford's mother decided it was improper for her to give birth to an illegitimate child in a film story. Finally Lubitsch settled upon *Don César de Bazan,* a French play by Adolphe d'Ennery and P. S. P. Dumanoir, which he had once discussed with Jesse L. Lasky as a possible vehicle for Rudolph Valentino. The rights had been bought by Lasky, who began making a version of it (*The Spanish Dancer*) with Pola Negri, but without Valentino. Due to a lapse of the rights, Lubitsch was able to arrange for their purchase by United Artists and he set about making exactly the same story under the title *Rosita,* working from a screenplay by Edward Knoblock who adapted an earlier version by Hans Kräly prepared in Europe.

Rosita was largely shot at San Diego, using the old Spanish buildings which still existed there. Lubitsch was uneasy with the subject and with American methods of production. He worked slowly, feeling thoroughly depressed. He refused to adapt his style of dress, and continued to wear very Germanic suits and ties, all of which looked entirely out of place and marked him to the employees of the studio as something of a "German tourist."

With the unfortunate experience of *Rosita* over, Lubitsch and Henry Blanke were called over to Famous

21

Players-Lasky, with whom they had a contract signed in Europe. Lubitsch told Lasky he was sick and tired of the factory system of making pictures in Hollywood. He asked Lasky to tear up the contract, and Lasky obliged, settling it with a substantial sum of money. Hearing this news on the grapevine, Harry Warner, who was determined to sign Lubitsch, decided on a ruse. He sent the lovely Irene Rich over to Lubitsch's house on Norton Avenue, to talk to him. The doorbell rang, and Lubitsch, glancing out of a window, saw the visitor. The ruse worked, and Lubitsch at once asked the lady in. "Harry Warner will come and see you in a few minutes," she said. When Harry Warner arrived, Lubitsch accepted his offer, looking most of the time at Irene Rich's legs. The contract gave him absolute carte blanche at all times, an agreement the Warners later had reason to regret.

At a series of meetings at the studio, Lubitsch laid down his policy to Jack Warner. He told him that he detested morbidity in art, and revolted fiercely against the trend, established now in Hollywood, of decadent romanticism, turgid photography, and overly elaborate sets. Maintaining that life was drab enough, he believed that films which reminded people too vividly of the sadness of the human condition would be certain failures. He wanted to show the delights and absurdities of life among the wealthy, the witty, the refined, while ignoring the cruelty, avarice and greed which made the maintaining of the lives of the rich a possibility. His films for Warners were mostly delicious escapist fantasies, satires on sex and financial success.

Jack Warner was, of course, not in the least interested in Lubitsch's aesthetic approach. Lubitsch's box-office figures in Europe had been impressive, and that was all Jack Warner was interested in. It was deeply shocking to Warner when he learned Lubitsch's conditions of work:

Lubitsch would not permit any of the Warner brothers on the set, except by special arrangement; his day's "rushes" (the uncut feet of film completed at the end of a day's work) would be sacrosanct and locked away in a specially padlocked metal closet; the cutting rooms were inviolate; and Lubitsch would cut every foot himself without the assistance of a studio editor. He insisted on absolute authority to select his cast and subjects, regardless of the preferences of his employers. Captivated by the German's prestige as a commercial film-maker, Jack Warner acceded to all these requests; but the worst problem of all later on did not lie in the vexatious terms of Lubitsch's contract, nor in the coolly amused and high-handed manner in which the German dealt with Jack's hard businesslike mind. It lay in the fact that Lubitsch was as spectacular a commercial failure in the American marketplace as he had been a success in the European one. Since the Warners could not tolerate even a genius who did not make money for them, their relations became excessively strained.

Shortly after his arrival at Warners, Lubitsch rented a large white house in Beverly Hills. It was designed in the colonial style, with a pillared portico (another white colonial house on the same street belonged to Pola Negri). Here he lived with Mrs. Leni Lubitsch and her two plump sons by a previous marriage. Mrs. Lubitsch decorated the house in a very "shop-window" fashion, with dull rococo and Louis XVI furnishings: the style was so meticulous that it amounted to no style at all. Leni was an extraordinarily attractive woman, fiercely sensual, with a face which invited men irresistibly; she wanted to conquer every man she met, driven as she was by an insatiable curiosity and hunger. Her "hunting look" frequently proved embarrassing at dinner parties. Men felt they were "on a pillory": she was assessing their physical appeal while Lubitsch watched her watching them, then observed their reaction to her. Wives were consumed with jealousy, and quarrels erupted when couples reached home.

Lubitsch tolerated Leni's behavior with a remarkable degree of good humor. Despite the constant backbiting and gossip-making of his social set (described by one of its members, because of its expatriate bitterness, as the *Sauer Crowd*), he bore her sexual liaisons with complete tolerance. However, he did not know of her affair with Hans Kräly, a constant visitor to his home for script conferences. Lubitsch and his wife literally lived out a Lubitsch film, a Schnitzler-like pattern of adultery and deceit.

Just at the moment when Lubitsch was settling into Warners, he was invited by Charlie Chaplin to see the first cut of Chaplin's *A Woman of Paris*, a sophisticated comedy of manners with Adolphe Menjou. After the screening Lubitsch walked up and down for an hour, and at once his entire approach to film direction changed: he would from now on devote himself to small-scale, infinitely detailed stories of interlocking lives, focusing on the minutiae of gesture.

The first film made with this policy in mind was entitled *The Marriage Circle*, adapted by Paul Bern from the play *Nur Ein Traum* by Lothar Schmidt. With Florence Vidor, Monte Blue, Marie Prevost and Adolphe Menjou, it was a deliciously amusing story of the entangled lives of two married couples. The film marked the beginning of Lubitsch's collaboration with a superb Warner cameraman: Charles Van Enger. Lubitsch had been having a problem with a sequence: Marie Prevost was seen bawling out Adolphe Menjou; impervious to her complaints, he was touching his toes, thrusting his buttocks up into her astonished face. Artificial sunlight was streaming through two windows of the room, on each side of him, causing a distracting shadow of Menjou's figure on the wall. Lubitsch asked Van Enger to solve the problem; Van Enger simply shone a light that seemed to come from another window which cast a shadow at an oblique angle.

Next day, when Van Enger arrived at the studio, Lubitsch told him he had achieved the quality he wanted and Van Enger took over *The Marriage Circle*. He brilliantly realized Lubitsch's effects: in particular a montage in which Marie Prevost and the chief members of the cast were shown in their various social poses, while *Ich Liebe Dicht* was played on the piano. Van Enger calculated with the director an exact count of feet of film needed to work out a series of extraordinarily rapid dissolves: 49 dissolves in 51 feet of film.

After the completion of *The Marriage Circle*, Jack Warner forced Van Enger to continue with Warners by blackmailing him: if he did not sign a year's contract with the studio he would be blacklisted in the industry. He became the leading cameraman at Warners, at $350 a week.

Lubitsch and Van Enger went to extraordinary lengths to provide a look of glamour on incredibly tight budgets. They would connive with the art department to give them doors and windows, curtains and chairs and charge them up to other productions in the budgets. Forced perspectives were used to still further enhance Harold Grieve's brilliant over-lifesize sets, painted "Grieve green" to give a shimmering grey quality on the screen; huge objects were used in the foreground and small objects in the background.

Lubitsch would work out the scenes of the film in his mind each night. In the morning, he would sit at his desk after breakfast and enjoy a cigar with Charles Van Enger, discussing in a relaxed manner the sequences to be shot that day. Then he would stroll onto the set, his hands behind his back, and instruct the technicians in preparing the scene for the appropriate camera positions. A com-

plete rehearsal of the players would follow at about nine
o'clock, with Lubitsch playing out every part. After they
were ready there would be another run-through of all
camera positions locked in to the precise movements of
the players. Only when every single detail was worked
out would Lubitsch proceed with a scene. He always
called off shooting at five o'clock, except where a night
location was indicated, as he wanted the players to be
completely relaxed. Aside from being sure that they knew
their lines, he told them to be at ease with their friends
and families in the evening, playing bridge or pinochle,
so that the following day they would be fresh and spar-
kling for the scene to come.

He developed a custom of serving coffee and cakes for
everyone at four o'clock each afternoon, supplied especially by a catering company. One day the coffee and cake
failed to arrive. Lubitsch asked James Flood, "Why?"
Flood said, "Jack Warner cancelled them." Lubitsch said
"All right," called off the day's work and went to his office to play the cello. Jack Warner came to him and said,
"What's happened to the shooting?" Lubitsch said, "No
coffee and cake, no scenes." Next day, the coffee and cake
were supplied exactly on time. On another occasion, Jack
Warner cancelled all the chairs used by the cast to prepare a scene. Lubitsch again repaired to his office to play
the cello, and when Warner stormed in he said gently,
"No chairs, no actors." Again Warner was defeated.

After *The Marriage Circle*, Lubitsch went on to make
Three Women, a masterpiece of social comedy, designed
by the great Sven Gaade, with Pauline Frederick at her
greatest in the role of a fading matron who fights bitterly
with her daughter for possession of a handsome young
man. Lubitsch, Kräly and Van Enger never equalled the
opening scene in which Miss Frederick weighs herself
gingerly on a pair of scales, makes up her sagging face,
and sails out of the house to a lavish ball, sliding down a

chute into the arms of an eligible bachelor. Few pictures have shown with equal precision the terror American women have of middle and old age. When Van Enger wanted to soften the photography of the star, Lubitsch instead made him take out all the shadows, put the lights low to emphasize the bags under Miss Frederick's eyes, and flood every inch of the set with light. The result was a visual presentation of merciless brilliance, acted out courageously by the star.

Of the films Lubitsch made for Warners, the most extraordinary was *Lady Windermere's Fan*, based by Julien Josephson on Wilde's play, without a single line of dialogue by Wilde used in the titles. Simply using the play as a point of departure for a contemporary story, the film was a masterpiece of wit and style. The finest sequence was that in which Mrs. Erlynne, played with great finesse by Irene Rich, is humiliated by a number of haughty society women at Ascot. Jack Warner wanted to shoot the sequence in a converted mudhole.

Lubitsch was furious: he had already decided to film the scenes in Canada. When Jack Warner yelled, "You son-of-a-bitch, why don't you film them in this country?" Lubitsch replied, "Because, *you* son-of-a-bitch, Canada's British and they race the horses in the opposite direction."

While Jack Warner became increasingly exasperated, the entire company left for Toronto, and filmed the race sequence there. At the conclusion of the shooting, Lubitsch said to Van Enger, "Charlie, we'll go to New York now, and have fun." His excuse to Jack Warner was that he had to take an extra closeup of Irene Rich. After Van Enger took the close-up at the Vitagraph studio, the company went to New York. One night, Van Enger took the actress Hope Drowne to the new play, *The Jazz Singer*, starring George Jessel; impressed, he urgently recommended it to Sam, Harry and Albert Warner, who went with Lubitsch to see the production. They decided simultaneously that it would not make a good picture. Van Enger insisted Lubitsch film it, and he agreed. It was in his contract that the studio buy any story he wanted, and he demanded they buy the play for him. Jack Warner was furious. He had to pay $250,000 for it. He called Van Enger into his office and yelled at him to "Mind your own goddamn business." As a result, Van Enger quit the studio.

Without Van Enger, Lubitsch began to lose heart at Warner Brothers. Aside from an elaborate Charleston sequence, his next film, *So This Is Paris*, was a disappointment to everyone, and in 1926, with scarcely a word to his employers, and ignoring his own insistence on making *The Jazz Singer*, he resigned and accepted a more substantial offer from Metro-Goldwyn-Mayer.

Aside from Lubitsch, the Warners' most substantial acquisition of the 1920s was John Barrymore. He was a man much closer to Jack Warner's heart than Lubitsch could ever be. For all his flamboyant affectiveness as an actor, he was a coarse-grained, fierce, heavy-drinking Lothario of the caliber Warner instantly admired.

The brothers had first seen Barrymore in his extraordinary performance in *Hamlet* for Arthur Hopkins at the Harris Theatre opening in New York on November 16, 1922, with Rosalind Fuller as Ophelia. They agreed with Hopkins' estimate: "Never was one man more blessed with all the attributes of the complex, towering, haunting Dane—beauty, grace, eloquence, humor, pathos and power." The reviews of the New York critics, including Alexander Woollcott and Heywood Broun, were very much in that vein. Jack Warner offered Barrymore a substantial contract.

Barrymore—who was planning to take the play to London—refused to sign it. But he signed a one picture agreement for *Beau Brummel* opposite the 17-year-old

Mary Astor who had been specially loaned by Paramount. He spent several weeks training Mary Astor in the art of acting at his suite at the Beverly Hills Hotel. They became very close: she recorded in her memoirs (*A Life on Film*) that he taught her she was "a person—and not just a Goddamn trained seal." She astounded him by her erudition: she told him and the director Harry Beaumont that the woman she was playing, Lady Margery Alvanley, never existed, and that Beau Brummel never fell in love with anyone "except himself." Despite the heat of the sets under the Cooper-Hewitt lights and the blazing Kliegs, the cast managed to play with extreme elegance in their heavy clothes, interrupted only, as Miss Astor recorded later, when Barrymore began talking obscenities to Willard Louis, playing the Prince of Wales.

After his British tour in *Hamlet*, Barrymore returned and signed a contract with the Warners which gave him the sum of $76,350 a picture and promised that the length of shooting of any picture would not exceed seven weeks. If it did, he would receive $7,625 for each additional week.

With his butler, Blainey, and his famous monkey Clementine, Barrymore swept into town and put up at the Ambassador Hotel, refurbishing at his own expense the suite set aside for him. Jack Warner begged him to make *Don Juan* as his first feature, but he thrust Warner's protests aside and proceeded instead to insist that he make a version of Herman Melville's Moby Dick, *The Sea Beast*.

The Sea Beast was a somewhat garbled version of Herman Melville's novel, a favorite book of Barrymore's. His performance as Captain Ahab was among the most mannered of his career. Each day he would drive from his rooms at the Ambassador Hotel to the harbor of San Pedro, where the director, Millard Webb, and the cinematographer, Lyman Broening, were waiting in a replica of the *Pequod* to take off into the ocean and shoot the ac-

tion scenes in heavy seas. In order to defend himself
against sea sickness and pneumonia, Barrymore invariably arrived on location very drunk. He was hastily
strapped up in his wooden leg, one leg bent painfully
behind him, yelling at the make-up men and costumers as
they fitted him into his awkward and ill-fitting clothes.
Once out on the *Pequod*, he quarreled constantly with
Webb and Broening. One afternoon, after an exceptionally heavy roll of the vessel, he crashed against a railing
and collapsed in agony, several ribs broken. He had to be
carried, shouting oaths, off the deck of the *Pequod* and
lowered by rope and pulley to a dinghy which rowed him
ashore. By the time he arrived he was soaked to the skin.
He had to be dragged on his sodden stretcher for several
feet when a wooden shaft snapped under his weight, and
the journey to the hospital by ambulance was a terrible
ordeal.

He returned from the hospital with his body ban-
daged. There was a sequence in which he had to attack
the mechanical whale with a large harpoon, stabbing a
special sac which would release red paint representing its
blood. He jumped overboard and began standing on the
whale, which threw him violently into the sea. He narrowly escaped being crushed between the boat and the
whale itself. Dragged aboard, he replayed the scene in
the teeth of a storm, with Millard Webb so soaked that his
megaphone filled with water. Then something went
wrong with the device which controlled the sac of imitation blood. A cable snapped back, the sac burst open, and
director, star and crew were soaked in the sticky crimson
substance.

The Sea Beast, despite the extreme unpleasantness of
its making, proved to be a success, and Barrymore was
firmly launched as a major Warner star. By 1925, he had
a rival, however: a four-legged rival. Alongside the "prestige pictures," the Lubitsch films, the versions of Sinclair

Lewis and Scott Fitzgerald, the Barrymore versions of Clyde Fitch and Melville, the Warners had not entirely forgotten their early work in the action field. And they now had an "action star" to beat them all. His name was Rin-Tin-Tin.

Rise of
the Dog Star

IT SEEMS AGREEABLY IRON-
ical that Rin-Tin-Tin, the most successful animal in
motion pictures, and the mainstay of Warners' financial
structure, was among the most disagreeable dogs who
ever lived. One of his co-stars, who wishes to be anonymous, has remarked: "He was literally and actually a son
of a bitch." Everyone who worked with this celebrated
quadruped is agreed that he was a monster: ill-tempered,
vicious, dangerous. He would attack members of the cast
without warning, savage his directors, and answer a
friendly pat with a menacing growl and perhaps a serious
bite. He was, in fact, the very model of a temperamental
Hollywood star, characteristic of the breed in every respect except one: he didn't drink. A long stream of articles
and at least two books gave the hagiography of the beast:

his gentleness and sweetness of character, his fondness for babies. The Rin-Tin-Tin publicity releases, in many cases fathered by Hal B. Wallis, a $50 a week studio publicity man, were accepted blindly by the press. The whole subject proved bitter amusement among the many employees of Warners who would like to have seen the creature shot: Charles Van Enger on one occasion even made an attempt on its life himself, after it gave him a particularly severe bite on his camera-cranking arm.

The dog's trainer, Lee Duncan, had found him as a puppy in a dugout during the Saint-Michel drive in France during the first World War. He had been abandoned together with a female, Nanette, by the Germans after a retreat. The name Rin-Tin-Tin was adapted from a nickname given by flyers to their good-luck yarn dolls dangling over the cockpit. Duncan imported both Nanette and Rin-Tin-Tin to New York; Nanette became ill and died. In Southern California, Duncan and a partner, the character actor Eugene Pallette, began to raise the dog and train it. In February, 1922, Rin-Tin-Tin entered his first dog show, winning a jumping event; in December of the same year, he appeared at the Hotel Ambassador Dog Show, earning loud applause as he sailed over a high bar, narrowly missing the diminutive actress Mary Miles Minter in the process. His photograph appeared in the *Los Angeles Times*, and several friends urged Duncan to place the dog in the movies.

Rin-Tin-Tin's first picture was *The Man from Hell's River*, directed by and starring Irving Cummings (later a distinguished director at 20th Century-Fox), for Cummings' own production company: a story of fur trading in the Canadian north, with plentiful dramatic events including a handsomely shot chase by sleigh. Cliff Smith's *My Dad*, made for R-C Pictures, was another tense affair with a similar wintry setting, and at Universal Rin-Tin-Tin was courageous again in Robert F. Hill's *Shadows of the North,* based on Edison Marshall's novel *The Skyline of Space,* with William Desmond and Virginia Brown. Later Lee Duncan wrote a story based on an old fairy tale, "Wellyn and His Dog," about a shepherd boy who was falsely suspected of killing a sportsman's son. When the outraged sportsman stabbed the dog, after discovering his son covered with blood, he found that his pet had in fact killed a wolf which had been about to tear the boy limb from limb. Duncan retitled the story *Where the North Begins.*

The story was rewritten by the author-director Chester Franklin, who sold it to the Warners. At an interview with Jack Warner, Duncan showed the dog's amazing ability to respond to direction. Its repertoire of tricks was seemingly limitless. Dog films were very popular at the time: the Strongheart series was proving a great success. A contract was drawn up, and the picture with Harry Rapf producing and Franklin directing, was made with Claire Adams and Walter McGrail as the human stars.

The story became in Franklin's hands a simpleminded affair about a German shepherd pup which is adopted by a wolf pack after being lost in a trek across Alaska. Grown up as a "wolf," Rin-Tin-Tin rescues a young French Canadian fur trapper and they become close friends. Shooting took place in the eternal snows of Truckee, in the High Sierras of California. Rin-Tin-Tin again proved a remarkable actor: brave, forceful, yet capable of suggesting pain, grief and fear. The only problem he presented due to Duncan's careful control was that of keeping him on the set: he twice ran off to pursue a fox. Jack Warner was delighted with him, and the preview at Glendale was a great success, with the dog in the audience to bark delightedly at himself.

At the premiere in Los Angeles, Rin-Tin-Tin walked onto the stage of the Loew's State Theatre and received enthusiastic applause as Duncan put him through some favorite tricks. A four-month promotional tour followed, in which Duncan and the dog visited countless hospitals and sanitariums, and appeared at many successive openings. On his return, Warners signed them to a three-year contract, and a very young writer named Darryl Zanuck devised a story for him. Zanuck was so determined to sell Jack Warner *Find Your Man* that he even got down on all fours in Warner's office, scratched, snarled, and ran up and down, giving a performance as Rin-Tin-Tin so effectively that Jack Warner cried with laughter. At once, the two men became close friends.

The director Jack Warner chose for the film was the tall and spindly, light hearted, and genial Mal St. Clair, later known as a director of Lubitsch-like, sophisticated comedies at Paramount. His cameraman was Lee Garmes, then at the outset of a career as one of the greatest cameramen in the history of Hollywood. With Zanuck, Lee Duncan, Rin-Tin-Tin, and the human cast, the unit went by train to Klamath Falls, Oregon, a shabby little town in pine forest country, with an Indian reservation at Fort Klamath nearby. There were two local movie theatres: the owner of both of them, Harry Poole, would run a reel of a film in one theatre, bicycle over to the other theatre so that the reel was run about 20 minutes later. Then he would cycle back to fetch reel number two. When the theatres ran a cowboy and Indian picture, the Indians from Fort Klamath would sit there all day long and gaze in a silent awe at the screen. If the accompanying feature was not a cowboy and Indian subject, they would troop outside, sit down on the curbstone and smoke. Then they would return to see the same picture round again, still hoping—in vain—that they would see themselves winning the battles on the screen.

The group enjoyed the clean air, brilliant sunlight and brisk breezes off the lake, and Rin-Tin-Tin acted superbly, protecting the hero and bringing down the villain, followed determinedly by Lee Garmes' ceaselessly panning Mitchell camera. Frequently, the company rose at dawn to shoot at Crater Lake, catching the first pale glitter of light on the water as Rin-Tin-Tin ran past dewy leaves and the last acrid dying smoke of travelers' campfires.

In one exciting scene, Rin-Tin-Tin had to deliver a note to a judge who was trying Eric St. Clair on a charge of stealing timber: after a run across country Rin-Tin-Tin was blocked at the door by a sheriff, clambered up on the roof, made his way down a chimney, and managed to leap up to the astonished judge with the note, forcing the true villain to make a confession before the court.

Mal St. Clair was really an "indoor" director at heart, and became impatient with the outdoor shooting and Rin-Tin-Tin's bad temper after the first three weeks. Zanuck suggested bringing in Roy Del Ruth to take over some of the second unit work, but St. Clair ruled that out completely: he and Del Ruth had both worked for Mack Sennett and an enmity existed between the two men. St. Clair screamed with rage at Zanuck for his suggestion and told him he was going to send him back home. Both St. Clair and Garmes had problems with the character actor who played the villain, Pat Hartigan. A rough-and-tough character, he had formerly been a New York policeman. He was constantly getting drunk, and on one occasion went into a barber shop and had his beard shaven off—when all of his scenes called for a beard. To enable the scenes to match, he had to have a false beard put on with glue. Often he had to be propped up below the frameline, with men gripping his legs to conceal the fact that he was practically falling over in a drunken stupor.

Despite Mal St. Clair's impatience and frequent rages, and the difficulties of matching Pat Hartigan's shots, the picture was finished on schedule, and Jack Warner was very pleased with it. The picture was released to excellent reviews, and became an immediate smash hit.

"Rinty" received upwards of 12,000 letters a week, and no self-respecting boy would be seen without a Rin-Tin-Tin badge pinned to his lapel. His face appeared on Ken-L-Ration's dog biscuit covers, he barked on radio, and several crackpots suggested he might be an embodiment of God. When he landed by plane at Roosevelt Field, New York, Grover Whalen met him with a police escort. He appeared at the Palace Theatre with Duke Ellington and his Cotton Club Orchestra, and proved he could bark in ragtime.

Rin-Tin-Tin's next feature, *The Lighthouse by the Sea*, was again directed by Mal St. Clair, adapted by Darryl Zanuck from Owen Davis' play, and starring William ("Buster") Collier and Louise Fazenda. Set in Maine, it was an exciting adventure story about a blind lighthouse keeper whose daughter, Flora (Miss Fazenda) had concealed the fact of the lighthouse keeper's infirmity, by doing his job herself. Albert Dorn (Collier) is shipwrecked with his dog, and he and Flora, who has effected his rescue, fall in love. Exciting events involve a team of bootleggers, who kidnap Flora, but Albert and Flora and their devoted canine help manage to foil the villains. The film was shot at Laguna Beach, which stood in for the rugged coastline of Maine.

The production cost, which caused Jack Warner and Motley Flint severe headaches, was $150,000: a fortune for the struggling studio in those days. Though the company cast was underpaid—Zanuck and Collier received $150 a week, and Hal Wallis $50 to Rin-Tin-Tin's $1000—no expense was spared to keep Rin-Tin-Tin happy: he even had a small orchestral group to keep him in the mood for the scenes, the finest Chateaubriand steaks to eat, and a collar with a diamond clasp.

After the first few days of shooting, Jack Warner fired Lee Garmes as cameraman and replaced him with Lyman Broening, who was presented with major problems on location at Laguna. Not only was Rin-Tin-Tin especially bad-tempered, even by his own standards, attacking several members of the cast and crew so that they were quite ready to kill him, but the lighting of the interiors of the lighthouse set was an extreme problem. The lighthouse, on its bluff over the sea, had to be lit so that the intense concentration of sunlight from outside exactly matched with the cooler light of the whitewashed rooms and the winding central staircase. Broening had to repaint the walls a more brilliant white, use filters on every aperture, and when a real storm broke (a godsend to the director, who thought it would have to be faked in the studio), he had to use alternating lights which matched the effect of flickering lightning on the walls.

In the scene in which Collier was washed ashore, with Rin-Tin-Tin at dusk, the cold was unbearably intense. When Rin-Tin-Tin began to shiver, Lee Duncan shouted a command and a launch came by with a number of crew members and the substitute, stand-in dog. Carefully wrapped in a blanket, Rin-Tin-Tin was carried like a parcel from Tiffany's into the launch, and the other dog jumped in next to Collier. Nobody, of course, cared about Collier's miserable discomfort: he was merely a human member of the cast. A moment later a particularly large wave overturned the boat and St. Clair ordered the cameraman Lyman Broening to continue shooting. Later in the picture, Rin-Tin-Tin attacked and bit several members of the crew who had to be forcibly restrained from killing him. St. Clair detested and despised the roaring melodrama of Zanuck's story, and kept adding tongue-in-cheek touches (in one scene, he had the dog operating the machinery to turn the light on and even mending a fuse) which infuriated the Warners.

After the successful completion of *The Lighthouse by the Sea*, Herman Raymaker directed Rin-Tin-Tin in *Below the Line*, with June Marlowe and Pat Hartigan brought back as heroine and villain, beautifully shot by John Mescall; Noel Mason Smith directed *Clash of the Wolves*, with a very young Charles Farrell in the cast; Herman Raymaker again directed *Tracked in the Snow Country*, with David Butler (later a noted Warner director) and June Marlowe, photographed by the great Ray June; and Raymaker excellently handled *A Hero of the Big Snows* and *The Night Cry*.

The formula of snowy landscapes, of wild seas, threats from wild-bearded trappers, kidnap and storm and terror seemed a little thin by 1926, and Jack Warner decided on a change of pace for the star dog. Herbert Bretherton's *While London Sleeps* was an excellent variation on the formula: Walter Morosco wrote the gripping screenplay and directed several sequences. The setting was a murky London, brilliantly photographed by Fred Kesson. Inspector Burke of Scotland Yard (played by DeWitt Jennings) is pursuing a killer called the London Letter (the sinister Otto Matieson) whose half-man, half-dog monster is the scourge of the back streets. Burke's daughter, Dale (Helene Costello) finds a way of destroying the villain by means of his own dog, Rin-Tin-Tin. The entire concoction had a powerful Germanic "dark" quality, quite unlike anything Rin-Tin-Tin ever did, and foreshadowed the Warner thrillers of later years.

Aside from the Rin-Tin-Tin series, the Warners made a number of exciting Western adventure epics in the mid-1920s, the most ambitious of which was *The Limited Mail*, written by Darryl Zanuck and Charles A. Logue, directed by George Hill, and photographed by Charles Van Enger. It was based on a comedy-drama, written in 1889, by Elmer Vance. The story involved the thrusting of the Limited Mail train across the West, with Monte Blue starring as Bob Wilson, a heroic engineer, whose great friend Tom Fowler, played by Tom Gallery, is killed when a runaway freight train crashes into the Limited.

39

Unhappy and disillusioned, Bob reverts to his former life as a hobo, but he prevents a train wreck when a tunnel collapses during a landslide, and again becomes a major legend of the railroad's epic story.

The unit travelled to Feather River to shoot a sequence in which one of the trains comes through 19 tunnels in 20 miles of track. The arrangement with the railroad was that when the unit assistant waved a white flag the train would come down the track. Meanwhile the electrically operated handcar carrying the camera unit was going up the track. Darryl Zanuck impetuously flagged down the train. The crew stood helplessly watching the handcar go up the track while the train came down it. It was impossible to give a signal. But then, for a completely unknown reason, the train fireman blew the whistle. The two prop men jumped off the handcar, tilted it over so that it slid down a slope into the Feather River, and then jumped after it. George Hill screamed at Zanuck, "You little rat-faced son of a bitch!" Zanuck started to run, and cameraman Charles Van Enger tackled Hill, saving Zanuck's life.

The unit then moved to Royal Gorge, in Canyon City, living entirely on a train. There, another mishap took place: the engine was being backed up a slope when it completely tipped over. On another occasion, the engine was started off so fast it went careening down a sharp curve, spilling off some of the crew as it did so.

The Limited Mail was a great success and between 1924 and 1927, Warners produced many exciting pictures of this kind. Meanwhile, their expansion as a major studio continued as a direct result of the success of these action films. Because of difficulty in obtaining satisfactory releases of their films, the brothers began, in September, 1924, a pattern of building theatres at a cost of $10 million, in Los Angeles, San Francisco, Portland, Seattle, Denver, Omaha, and in several Canadian cities. Harry Warner issued a statement on September 9, 1924:

"Warner Brothers is an independent concern, and, despite the efforts of others interested in the industry, we are determined to show the public our pictures. We are building our own theatres for that purpose. Ever since we have been in the film-producing business we have operated on an independent basis, and I believe we are now in a position to take this step for the protection of our interests.

"It is not through any wish on our part to enter the exhibiting end of the industry, but it is a protective measure to ourselves and the exhibit that we plan the construction of this string of theatres. The situation has become serious for us."

In February, 1925, radio station KWBC ("Warner Brothers Classics") was installed at the Sunset Boulevard studio at a cost of $50,000. It was developed with the aid of a Major Nathan Levinson, who had been a consultant to Theodore Roosevelt during the period of his presidency, and was now a sales representative of Western Electric. On March 3, the first program was a recital by a baritone singer, "Leon Zuardo"; Leon Zuardo was in fact none other than Jack Warner himself.

On April 23, the brothers completed the purchase for three million dollars, of the Vitagraph Studio, including an extensive outfit in Flatbush, New York, and in Hollywood, a studio and laboratory at 1708 Talmadge Avenue, in addition to 50 distribution exchanges—26 in the United States, 4 in Canada, 10 in England and 10 in continental Europe. Warners also acquired 18 years of Vitagraph films, going back to the company's first production, *The Black Diamond Express*, made in 1898. Albert E. Smith and J. Stuart Blackton of Vitagraph temporarily joined the board of directors of Warners. That spring, the company was making vociferous charges of gross monopolizing of the industry by the "Big Three," M-G-M, Associated First National, and Famous Players-Lasky. They charged—

together with other members of the Independent Producers' Association—that the "Big Three" sought a monopoly of the motion picture industry by combining production and distribution with exhibition. At a convention
of independent exhibitors in Milwaukee, on May 13–16,
attended by 1500 motion picture theatre owners, the
issues were thoroughly thrashed out. In an impassioned
speech, Harry Warner demanded that Marcus Loew of
M-G-M, Adolph Zukor of Famous Players-Lasky, and Al
Rockett of First National should "lay their cards on the
table" regarding the monopoly issue. Irving Thalberg of
M-G-M and Al Rockett both denied that any trust or combine existed among the producers, but Harry Warner, who
had experienced violent opposition to his booking of films
into theatres, knew differently.

The Los Angeles Times commented on the whole situation: "Underlying the whole fight between the producers, this fact seems to stand out, as pointed to by
various executives: An independent producer produces
two films, let it be assumed. One is a nationally acclaimed
success, the other an ordinary picture. A syndicate in control of production and theaters is willing to accept the success but will give one of its own productions preference
over the ordinary film. But on the ordinary film probably
depends the life of the independent producer. No producer can make every picture a marvel."

Harry Warner said that combines like West Coast Theaters were spreading to smaller towns. "In these cases
where these affiliations exist, it is the common practice of
the Big Three to throw the fear of God into the individual
independent exhibitor and to force him to buy their specific product in preference to any other. He has no alternative, for it is a relatively simple matter for the larger
outfit to build in opposition to him and eventually to put
him out of business unless he books their pictures."

Jack Warner said: "At no time will our company build

theaters in opposition to another showman where our product is receiving equal showing with productions of other producers. It is not our intention to go into the show business in opposition to those already established and showing our pictures. At this Hollywood Theater we will show not only our own productions, but those of other producers, the policy being to show the best pictures available."

The theatre would cost $1,250,000 and seat 3600. A ballroom, a roof garden and promenade, and shops and offices were also planned. There would be facilities for elaborate stage productions, and the orchestra pit would seat 100 musicians. The radio station would be transferred to the theater. *The Los Angeles Times* said: "The theater, it is announced, will make Warner Brothers the only organization to produce, print and exhibit its pictures in Los Angeles."

On May 16, the Big Three case continued. Fred W. Beetson, secretary of the Motion Picture Producers and Distributors of America, an organization headed by Will H. Hays, called Warner's attack on the Big Three "just a case of publicity-seeking by an organization that hopes to attract attention to itself through attacking successful companies."

Warner replied, using the theater situation in Los Angeles as an example of the exhibition situation in the whole country:

"The Metropolitan Theater, Grauman's Million Dollar Theater, and the Rialto are all owned or controlled by Paramount Company. The West Coast theaters, who own the First National franchise on the Coast, as well as being part owners of the First National franchise in Greater New York, operate Loew's State Theater under a contract with Metro-Goldwyn-Mayer. They operate the Criterion, the California, Millers, the Alhambra and I understand a deal has been made whereby Grauman's Million Dollar

Theater has just been or will shortly be turned over to the West Coast. The West Coast even owns a half interest in Grauman's Egyptian Theater located in Hollywood."

Warner continued by saying that West Coast recently bought the Cameo Theater: several Vitagraph pictures were booked at the theater, and were cancelled when ownership changed.

"In the Los Angeles situation, all of the theaters downtown are owned or controlled through arrangements and affiliations with the West Coast and Famous Players, where all their pictures are played and none other except on rare occasions."

On May 16, Universal, Mary Pickford, Douglas Fairbanks, and Charlie Chaplin announced that $500,000 was being contributed for publicity to support independent exhibitors vs. the "Big Three."

The same day Harry Warner made another statement on the controversy: "We invite members of the Big Three to sit in open meeting with us and show their plans for exhibition of pictures in their theaters for the coming year. The public will then see the plans that have as their goal the elimination of the independent producer and exhibitor.

"We independents charge there is a solid combine which prevents the outsider from doing business with his product. Independent producers are not getting first runs and our assertion that there is a trust is answered only by half-hearted and vague replies from some of the minor executives and employees but there has not been a word from the heads of the companies alluded to."

Harry Warner added that he was annoyed by a rumor circulating at the theatre owner's convention in Milwaukee which alleged that Warners was affiliated with M-G-M, and that M-G-M provided the money for Warner Brothers' purchase of Vitagraph.

"We brand that as a malicious lie," Warner said, "and

I will give $100,000 to charity if anyone can show we are affiliated in any way to Metro-Goldwyn-Mayer or any other interests."

From their violent opposition to the "Big Three" and the thrust into the theatre field, it was obvious that the Warners intended rivalling M-G-M and Paramount (Famous Players-Lasky) in the future. In this they had the wholehearted support not only of Motley Flint, but, in New York, of the powerful Goldman, Sachs and Company, one of whose directors, a film enthusiast named Waddill Catchings, actually joined the Warners board in 1925. On October 25, 1925, a banking group led by Goldman, Sachs made a four million dollar note issue of Warner Brothers stock in order to expand the Warners program. On January 3, 1926, Harry Warner, Jack Warner, the new 29-year-old head of production Bennie Ziedman and the omnipresent Motley Flint officiated at the ground-breaking ceremony of the Warner Theatre at Hollywood and Wilcox.

Motley Flint broke the ground with a golden spade. Then, through the large crowd, a hearse with nodding black plumes arrived, accompanied by two men in pitch-black mourning with stovepipe hats. A sign on the hearse read, "Success to Warner Brothers, Sid Grauman." * Later that day Harry and Jack sent for a dummy from their studio and dressed it up as Sid Grauman, burying it with all ceremony in a plot on Hollywood Boulevard. Over it they placed a sign reading, "Here lies King Sid Grauman. Your hair will wave no more."

Despite all the grand announcements, the building plans, the lavish investments, the Warners were in fact in severe financial difficulties. No sooner had they completed a new building than they borrowed money on it to

* Sid Grauman was the most celebrated theatrical showman in Los Angeles, whose famous Chinese Theater was to open the following year.

build another. Soon their resources were stretched beyond the limit. In their earnest attempt to become a major studio, they began to find their accounts so overdrawn that checks they paid to their employees continually bounced. Moreover, they forced their employees to buy Warner stock. Quite frequently the value of the stock fell so low that employees found themselves in severe financial difficulties. Most extraordinary of all, employees were sometimes asked to contribute to the cost of a production, causing extreme hardship in many cases.

In November, 1925, Harry Warner and Motley Flint left for Europe, announcing that they would be making pictures in Germany and France, and signing up a brilliant young Hungarian director, Michael Curtiz, who had just enjoyed a great success with a production of *Moon of Israel,* from the novel by H. Rider Haggard. When Curtiz, a dashing, malapropish, colorful and somewhat piratical genius of the romantic film, arrived in New York, an immense crowd was out on the New York wharves, with flags flying and fireworks going off. "How fantastic! All for me!" he cried out. "I'm sorry to disillusion you, Mr. Curtiz," said a Warner executive standing beside him at the rail, "but it's the Fourth of July."

In the meantime, Sam, who had remained in New York when his brothers went to Europe, had become involved in a widely publicized romance. Earlier that year, Sam had been to a party at the home of Victor Watson, publisher of the *New York American:* there he had met a ravishing 17-year-old girl, Lina Basquette, who was appearing with Florenz Ziegfeld's company. He wanted to marry her at once. Though she was not attracted to him, her mother and stepfather urged her to marry him for his money. She bent to their wishes, and the marriage took place at 7 PM on July 5, 1925, at the New York home of Dr. Nathan Krass of Temple Emanu-El who performed the Jewish ceremony. Motley Flint was the best man.

Bernard Sobel, the famous Ziegfeld press agent, played the Wedding March on the piano, and among those present were Leon Errol and Pauline Mason, who were in the cast of Ziegfeld's *Louie the XIV* with Miss Basquette; Ziegfeld's business manager, Samuel Kingston; and the silent film vamp Louise Glaum. After attending the performance of the Follies that night, the couple and their guests went to the Biltmore Cascades, where George Olsen's Orchestra played an extemporaneous program. Miss Basquette sang a number of tunes especially composed for the occasion by Louis Gress. Constance Bennett officially welcomed the party and Corinne Griffith gave the bride a corsage of orchids arranged by herself.

Not only was Sam's future bullish at Warners in 1925 and early 1926, but the greatest excitement of all at the studio in those days was stirred up by the brothers' commitment to an extraordinary gamble. They were going to revive an old dream of the motion picture industry: the dream of sound.

"Sound Holds
No Terrors
for Rin-Tin-Tin"

ALMOST FROM THE BE-
ginning of the industry, sound films had been an hallucinatory vision of motion picture makers. Thomas Alva
Edison in 1911 had attempted synchronization without
any great degree of success. In 1914 a fire at his plant
destroyed all of his equipment. Six years later his West
Coast engineers, Orlando Kellum and Brian Battey, financed by a New York financier named Wendell McMa-
hill, managed to achieve some sound effects, words, and a
song as an accompaniment to D. W. Griffith's production
of *Dream Street*. This was not successful: the screening in
May, 1921, at the New York Town Hall was greeted with
silent disapproval by the audience. It was left to a determined inventor, Lee De Forest, to pursue the dream in
the wake of Griffith's disappointment. He demonstrated

his Phonofilm in Berlin on August 16, 1922: it was a device whereby sound was photographed directly onto a strip of film. The Phonofilm was well received, and back in the United States, De Forest began experimenting with synchronized music and speech, engaging as his collaborator the distinguished musical arranger and conductor Dr. Hugo Riesenfeld. His first demonstration of a synchronized musical track was used at a premiere of *Bella Donna*, with Pola Negri in the title role, at the Rivoli Theatre in New York on April 15, 1923.

Simultaneously, De Forest managed to convince Calvin Coolidge that talking-film appearances would considerably enhance his "image" in his presidential campaign. Coolidge's defeated rival, John W. Davis, also used the Phonofilm as an electioneering device, and on January 16, 1926, Edwin Markham, author of that popular Poem "The Man with a Hoe," read his poem on Phonofilm at a special ceremony at the Smithsonian Institute in Washington.

Meanwhile, Western Electric, working in conjunction with the Bell Telephone Laboratories in New York, had been developing sound-on-disc synchronization with film for some time. This was more satisfactory than De Forest's techniques. The Bell Laboratories had been experimenting with accoustical recordings and with public address systems, but the sound-on-film idea was a comparatively recent development. Nathan Levinson had tried to sell it to all of the film companies, but none was interested except Warners. In 1925 he finally managed to persuade Sam Warner to come to New York and see a demonstration reel.

Levinson explained to Sam Warner the principle of the technique: Two motors were used, held at the same speed by an electric gear. The motors were interconnected by slip rings so that there was sufficient interchange of power between the armatures to produce synchronization while starting. Synchronization was then

49

maintained by the frequency of the power source (which determined the speed of both motors).

In reproducing, the film and sound machine were coupled to opposite ends of the same motor. The motor speed was held constant by a vacuum tube regulator. A flywheel device prevented mechanical vibrations and irregularities of tone from changing the speed of the record.

As Sam sat in a darkened room at the Bell Laboratories, Nathan Levinson ordered the projector started. Warner found himself looking at a living room scene: a man coming through a door, strolling over to a table, removing a straw hat and putting it down, unbuttoning his white kid gloves and placing them nearly inside the hat. Each sound in turn was synchronized with the movements on the screen. Finally, the man said a few words, and a violinist and a piano provided a duet. The man began to sing.

The technique was simple: a long-playing record, 16 inches across, was played simultaneously with the film. The original material was recorded in the same manner normally used in a phonograph studio.

Harry, Albert and Jack were at first skeptical. Jack Warner recalls in his memoirs * that Sam had to trick Harry into accepting a fake appointment with several Wall Street financiers at the Bell Laboratories, where he showed him a musical short he had prepared himself.

Harry was impressed, and the decision was made jointly with Sam to proceed at once. A man named Walter Rich had obtained an option from the Western Electric Company for the commercial development of talking-picture apparatus, and Warners immediately obtained a half interest in the Rich contract. The indispensable friend of Harry Warner, Waddill Catchings of Goldman, Sachs, arranged for his company to advance underwrite a

---

* *My First Hundred Years in Hollywood: An Autobiography.* Jack Warner with Dean Jennings, Random House, 1964.

$4,200,000 note issue. The purchaser of each $1000 note received an option to obtain at maturity $1050 plus 7½ shares of Warner common stock. Fifty thousand shares of common stock was needed to cover the financing, 30,000 to cover the bonus accompanying the notes and 20,000 to compensate the underwriters. The 50,000 shares of bonus stock was the price which the corporation had to pay for borrowing $4,200,000 for three years at 6½ percent. These 50,000 shares came from the brothers' personal holdings, when Catchings told them it was not possible for the company to issue additional stock. As a result of these arrangements, Western Electric Company granted an exclusive license to the Vitaphone Corporation whose stock was owned by Warners and Rich. And for over two years, from 1926 to 1928, since the company was in so parlous a state it could not obtain loans, the brothers simply lent it the money to see it over the hump into sound, to a total of $5,604,250 in guarantees.

On April 26, 1925, the Warners and the Western Electric Company jointly announced that after research at the Bell Laboratories they had decided to try the invention. "It will bring," they said, "to audiences in every corner of the world the music of the greatest symphony orchestras and the vocal entertainment of the most popular stars of the operatic, vaudeville and theatrical fields." They added, shrewdly, that the new device could also be used in "the educational, commercial and religious fields," thereby opening a whole new range of marketing possibilities.

On June 17, 1926, they announced a policy of "movie grand opera" which would "bring the Metropolitan to Main Street," and they bought the Piccadilly Theater in New York, converting it to the Warner Theater.

Like De Forest, even they did not at first see the talking film as a means of bringing spoken drama to the public. Instead, it seemed to them that its best use would be in musical shorts, and in promotional announcements. They therefore proceeded to arrange a contract with the Metropolitan Opera Company for the exclusive release of some of its stars, whom Sam Warner, with the aid of a Western Electric team, a Met director and the photographer Ed DuPar, shot at the Vitagraph studio in Brooklyn, singing some of their most popular arias, while Victor supplied the matching records. Since these shorts would not attract sufficiently large audiences on their own— public and press had long since grown out of their original excitement at De Forest's showing—they had, clearly, to be combined with a major feature, in the same way that De Forest's Phonofilm debut at the Rivoli had preceded a showing of *Bella Donna*.

Immediately, Jack Warner and Bess Meredyth, the doyenne of West Coast female scenarists, decided to construct a lavish vehicle for John Barrymore, *Don Juan*, to follow the now rapidly dubbed Warner Vitaphone shorts. And in addition, a special *Don Juan* score was commissioned from Dr. William Axt, to be supervised by David Mendoza and the famous Amateur Hour compere Major Edward Bowes.

The filming of *Don Juan* in Hollywood and of the Vitaphone shorts in New York took place simultaneously in 1925. To direct *Don Juan*, Jack Warner chose the 31-year-old Alan Crosland, then the studio's most successful box office director. A former journalist and theatre critic, energetic, tense, suave, Crosland had talked his way into a first assignment at the age of 21, making a comedy whimsically entitled *Santa Claus vs Cupid*. Other successes followed: a version of Robert Louis Stevenson's *Kidnapped; The Flapper*, a Lionel Barrymore vehicle; *The Enemies of Woman*, a version of Stanley Weyman's historical romance *Under the Red Robe;* and *Compromise*, a melodrama with Irene Rich. The Warners trusted him with the new vehicle partly because of his hero worshipper's friendship with John Barrymore—they were frequent heavy drinking partners—partly because he knew how to handle action and women stars (Barrymore wanted his mistress Dolores Costello cast, but the studio preferred a comparative newcomer, Mary Astor).

Don Juan abandoned history for a series of quietly spoofed, violent and dramatic episodes which could be filmed with the minimum of subtlety and the maximum of speed. Since the film had to be finished in time for its Brooklyn scoring and matching in 1926, it was shot through night after night, the cast frequently called back later the next morning after a 5:00 AM to 9:00 AM break.

Mary Astor has recorded in her memoirs that she was bent backwards over a wheel in the torture scenes so often and for such long periods she suffered severe pain in the neck and back. The cameraman, Byron Haskin (then Haskins) and Crosland had to go down in an airtight iron box to film the submarine sequence when, with the aid of a loosened brick and a deranged fellow prisoner, Don Juan escapes from an Italian prison into a tributary of the Tiber; they almost suffocated when something went wrong with the apparatus.

Barrymore forced the production to proceed as long as possible, because his contract specified that for every day he made the picture over a certain period, he would be paid triple time. His drunkenness often created more delays. In one scene he had to climb a trellis, rush into Mary Astor's bedroom and take her in his arms. He insisted upon wearing for the scene a voluminous white cape which he wound around his body, unravelling it at the crucial moment. In front of a crowd of important set visitors, including Louella Parsons, he climbed up the trellis, twirled the cloak with an air of dramatic passion—and fell flat on his face before the astonished Mary Astor.

Fifty-three period doors, built into the sets, had a tendency to jam, placing the actors in frequent embarrassing predicaments. In a scene representing authentically the dungeons of the Castel Sant Angelo, a special fog machine created a noisome gaseous substance to convey a feeling of subterranean slime and foulness. A sort of powder was also used, fine grained and scattered like pepper to create a look of swarming smoke. The effect of these substances was to force the actors off the set for several minutes at a time to gulp for air. Barrymore's drunken state proved an advantage in getting through these scenes, but he had to sober up in one shot which called for him to remain under water forty-eight seconds, and to manage a gigantic and later famous leap from the top of a staircase onto the neck of his enemy Donati (Montagu Love, snarling villainously) halfway down.

Back East in Brooklyn, the problems were equally agonizing. Supervised by the Bell engineer Stanley Watkins, the small Vitaphone sound stage was alive with microphones which were hidden everywhere out of camera range: in bowls of flowers, telephones, cigar boxes and bouquets held by the singers. Sam Warner, directing, was unable to utter a sound. If he wanted to move behind the camera, he had to do so in stockinged feet. The slightest noise—birds fluttering on the studio's glass roof, the patter of rain, the rumble of the subway, even the faint whirr of the camera—was unavoidably recorded on the slowly turning 16 inch discs. The singers and musicians were practically stationary, but when it came to recording a comedy act and the player needed to move to stress a point, his voice came out faintly at one moment, loudly at another.

Fortunately, the team working with Sam Warner managed to devise a control board which could be used to affect drastic variances in volume. But the irritations still vexed Sam: every time a record was played back some noise that no one had previously detected would come through, ruin a take, and force an unfortunate Met star to reject the same performance a tenth or eleventh time. The minutest rehearsal became necessary, a box had to be built to house the camera, and mattresses and horse blankets were optimistically tacked to the walls to muffle echoes.

Working with Warner, a group of experts including Stanley Watkins and George Groves consulted every day in order to work out different technical aspects of the shooting. One man was in charge of the perfect synchronization of image and sound. Another worked on the alternating camera system, working at how to transfer from long shots to close-ups. Yet another figured out the precise increase in volume necessary when a face moved from medium to full close-up within one shot. Makeup men, optics specialists and enunciation coaches milled around the cramped, freezing studio space all that winter, arguing incessantly until Sam Warner's nerve almost broke.

In addition to the musical shorts, Sam Watkins and the Bell Telephone people were preparing sample comedy-sketch films featuring vaudeville artists, including the celebrated George Jessel. But despite the tension involved, Sam Warner was driven on. He even survived the hazardous business of matching the score specially composed by Axt, played by the New York Philharmonic and matched by stopwatch to the images of *Don Juan* as the epic arrived reel by reel from the West Coast.

In an interview with *The New York Times* in 1925, Sam looked forward tensely and nervously to the new era. "We might," he said, "take a Broadway drama, word and action, exactly as it is presented on the stage and reproduce it without change, providing that the actors . . . screened well. We might make a hybrid of it. That is, we might start by filming some of the story in the exterior sets and working up to the spoken drama.

"If this form of entertainment becomes popular it will create a new specialty—dialogue writing. There will be no more titles. Dialogue writing will not be exactly the same art that it is in the legitimate drama. The scenario will be only the foundation for films of this type."

Sam had, he told the *Times*, spent the nights tossing restlessly, wondering about the problems of finding suitable actors for talking films. He knew that stage actresses might often not be perfectly photogenic. Hundreds of these had insufficiently regular features for the camera. A beauty queen he tested looked too hard-bitten when filmed. "The camera searches out defects the eye does not detect—a slightly pointed nose, a droop to the jaw," he told the *Times*. Moreover, he foresaw that the existing stars, many of them young and poorly educated or foreign, would not record well on sound. For the problem of stage players—and especially opera stars—who lacked photogenic glamor and for screen players with great beauty and miserable voices, there seemed no certain solution. And not even dubbing would do.

When the *Times* asked Warner if he might, perhaps, consider grafting the voice of some great stage actress with the face of imported sirens like Greta Nissen and Pola Negri, he said flatly: "It would never work." The audience, he felt, would "smell a rat," and the technique would throw severe strains on an actor who would stand there mouthing while someone else uttered the words that gave the illusion of a golden voice. And Warner added a final, wry note: "Suppose the thing *could* be faked. What a battle there would be between the face and the voice for money!

"The voice might start at a nominal figure. Later on, after the combination had become a great popular favorite, the voice could hold up the face for 50 per cent. If the voice went on strike, the face would be ruined. A great motion picture star might have a deep bass in one scene and a mellow baritone in another."

These problems, novel and painful as they were, existed in the future. Early in 1926, Sam Warner had to contend with a new problem: gelignite blasts for a subway extension directly under the sound stage had so much impact they jolted the needles off the matching disc grooves.

Finally, the fraying thread of his patience snapped. Quite suddenly, and halfway through shooting the Vitaphone shorts, Warner took a year's lease on Oscar Hammerstein's Manhattan Opera House on 34th Street and transferred his players there. The stage was extended over the auditorium, the boxes became equipment rooms. Mary Garden's old dressing room was made over to house electric generators. The stifling heat of the hottest summer in twenty years made the perspiration run down the faces of the singers and orchestra players, ruining their makeup.

One serious problem was that there was no way of editing sound; every sequence had to be shot with a full 10-minute roll of film. The discs were 16 inches in diameter, and ran at 33-⅓ rpm, some 25 years before the speed standard for long playing records. They were solid blocks of wax, about two inches thick and very highly polished; after a recording was finally approved, the disc was sent out to be copperplated. The matrix was used for records which were sent out to theatres across the country.

Under the direction of George Groves, the monitor room for mixing all of the sound was on the sixth floor of the building and served also as a Masonic Shrine Room. All the wire from the stage had to be fed to the monitor through the ventilation ducts; the mixing panel was mounted on the grill whence the ventilating air emerged; at the end of the day this massive equipment had to be removed to permit the masonic meetings to take place. During one recording session a thunderstorm broke out, causing so much static electricity in the monitor room that the entire work for the day was ruined.

Eddie DuPar told the *American Cinematographer*

(September, 1926) his techniques of making these musical shorts: "The microphones are so sensitive that we can detect if anybody on the set makes the least noise, such as walking, whispering or even the flickering of a light. If such are recorded, then the record is ruined. A flicker of a light sounds out like a pistol shot. This makes for a severe test on the lights. A number runs about ten minutes, or between 900 and 1000 feet. On some I have to use big storage batteries, weighing about 400 pounds each; seven of them are required to run a G. E. light of 150 amps. I use batteries to avoid generator noise. On the same lights, we had the gears changed from metal to fiber in order to eliminate gear noise on the automatic feed light.

"Since beginning this work," DuPar stated, "I have almost remodelled my camera. I use 1000 foot magazines, high-speed shutter, leather belt, special clutches on the take-up spool, and a light signal built right in the camera.

"A strange incident occurred when we were taking 'Swanee River.' Everything was still, and I had just received the signal to start; I flashed back the signal that I was fading in and everything was going nicely when I noticed frantic signals to stop. Looking out the peek-hole, I saw that everyone was exceedingly excited. The cause, I learned, had been the screams of a colored janitress who claimed that she had seen the late Oscar Hammerstein walking across the balcony. It was eleven o'clock in the morning, and it is said that it was his old custom to walk across the balcony at that time in the old Manhattan Opera House which we were using to work in. This was the third time that the janitor's force had claimed seeing Mr. Hammerstein, and of course the commotion ruined that shot."

At last the immense task of filming the Vitagraph Vitaphone shorts had reached the end of its initial stage: sufficient shorts were available to make a supporting program for *Don Juan,* and the *Don Juan* score was fully matched up.

"Sound Holds No Terrors for Rin-Tin-Tin"

The premiere of *Don Juan* took place at the Broadway Theatre in New York on August 8, 1927. A radio commentator in the lobby noted the society figures arriving: despite the excitement of the revived Hall-Mills murder case—two suspects were arrested the same day—the investigations into the fanancier Samuel Insull, and the startling news that thirty-seven people had died of a heat wave, the Warner publicity machine had ensured the audience was still passionately concerned with only one thing: seeing sound movies born.

Vitaphone was listed as the star, above John Barrymore's name, and dwarfing it. Warners spent a fortune on decorations for the house. A cardboard sign showed John Barrymore, the Great Profile, as Don Juan embracing Mary Astor in a foam of pink-edged cumulus cloud. Female nudes shone, spelled out in lobby lights that flickered alternately pink and blue, suggesting the varying pulsations of sound. The entire staff, including the manager, was dressed in 15th-century costumes, many made over from the wardrobe worn in the film.

The audience included several of the musical figures to be featured, and Will H. Hays, President of the Motion Picture Producers and Distributors of America. (The stars had been held in reserve for the West Coast premiere.) As the curtains parted, the image showed Hays, weasel-faced, narrow-shouldered, thin and precise, stepping up to praise, in his unpleasant hoosier twang, the splendors of Western Electric, the Bell Telephone Company, and the brothers Warner, reading his lines all too obviously off an idiot board. The audience applauded politely rather than ecstatically, and the image changed—to the New York Philharmonic under conductor Henry Hadley, vigorously rendering Wagner's *Tannhauser* Overture, which rather hollowly resounded into every part of the auditorium.

Marion Talley, then the toast of New York as star of the Met, now almost totally forgotten, sang Gilda's aria

"Caro Nome," from Act I of *Rigoletto*. Roy Smeck, the vaudeville comedian whose dubbing sessions had given Sam Warner his severest headaches, played a guitar and delivered himself of a monologue, "His Pastimes." Anna Case sang "La Fiesta," with accompaniment by the Cansino dance group, including a beautiful child named Marguerita Cansino, later to be known as Rita Hayworth. Mischa Elman played the violin. Efrem Zimbalist provided variations on Beethoven's the *Kruetzer* Sonata. Giovanni Martinelli sang the closing Act I aria from *Pagliacci*, "Vesta la Giubba," and the Philharmonic brought the proceedings to a vigorous close with national song medleys.

The audience was impressed, applauded loudly after each single film—and yet failed to respond as ecstatically as the Warners had hoped.

Don Juan's sound effects proved more exciting: the pealing of bells provoked cheers as the sound accompanied the wedding of Don Juan and Adriana Della Varnese, crowd scenes roared and duel scenes were heard in resounding clashes of steel. The music, a potpourri based on William Axt's reliable program compositions *The Fire Adagio* and *In Gloomy Forests* and the works of several French composers, was less impressive, and several observers remarked that a live orchestra or a celestial Wurlitzer would have been a great deal more desirable than the somewhat thin sounds produced by the Philharmonic for the occasion.

But if the public failed to be overwhelmed, the press went completely overboard. Mordaunt Hall of *The New York Times* voiced the city's opinion when he wrote of Mischa Elman: "Every note that came to one's ears synchronized with the gliding bow and the movements of the musician's fingers. It seemed at times that the sound was so distinct that during a pause"—Hall was scarcely notable for his original use of language—"had a pin been dropped in the studio it would have been heard." On Martinelli he waxed lyrical: "The singer's tones appeared to echo in the body of the theatre as they tore from the shadow on the screen—a shadow that appeared earnest and intense in the delivery of Leoncavallo's well-known composition."

Though *Don Juan* itself was—to the chagrin of Alan Crosland and Barrymore—overshadowed by the program which preceded it, there was no question that the evening was a triumph of prestige for Warner Brothers.

Soon after the West Coast premiere at Grauman's Egyptian Theater, *Variety* came out with an entire issue on the Vitaphone—the proof that, though the public was barely aware of it—the greatest revolution since pictures began had gotten off to a vigorous start. But it was only a beginning; and almost at once the Warners were up against a formidable problem.

5

Rivalries

ILLIAM FOX WAS THE problem: the head of the Fox Film Corporation had in 1925 bought the German Tri-Ergon process, in which sound was recorded directly onto film by means of a photoelectric cell. The creators of Tri-Ergon were three struggling young German inventors: Hans Vogt, Joseph Massolle, and Jo Engel. As early as 1912, Vogt, then 22, and an engineer in the navy, developed some primitive sound-on-film devices. After World War I, he and his two colleagues managed to work out a system of transferring sound onto film and developed an advanced loudspeaker system. They staged their first demonstrations in 1922, at about the same time Lee De Forest showed his primitive device in Berlin.

In 1923, the three inventors sold their entire interest

in their newly entitled Tri-Ergon system to a Swiss lawyer named Curti for a million francs. Curti was bought out by three Swiss combines in 1923, and in 1925 UFA, the German film studios, actually produced a Tri-Ergon talkie two years ahead of *The Jazz Singer: The Girl with the Matches (Des Mädchen Mit den Schwefelholzern)*. It was a disaster; the sound was disagreeably shrill and ill-matched. UFA cancelled its Tri-Ergon contract, and the Tri-Ergon Company came to a standstill.

It was at that awkward moment in the company's fortunes that W. T. Case, a former associate of Lee De Forest's, stepped in for Fox and bought the American Tri-Ergon rights for 200,000 francs (about $66,000 in the United States). Wisely, William Fox decided to give sound on film a trial run, not in features, but in his famous Movietone newsreels.

On Friday, April 29, 1927, convinced of the superiority of sound on film over sound on disc, he displayed the world's first talking newsreel at a private showing for the press in the largest theatre in the United States—his sumptuous "Cathedral of the Cinema," the Roxy, in which he had acquired a five million dollar controlling interest.

The lights in the famous wrought iron brackets dimmed, the curtains with their rich tableaux parted, and the small black and white square in the middle of the world's largest proscenium flickered into life. Isolated in the middle of Roxy's 6000 seats, the tiny knot of newsmen leaned forward excitedly. As a long-distance shot of the United States Military Academy at West Point faded in, General March B. Stewart delivered a speech about the life of the cadets under his tutelage in a voice completely unaffected by the hollowness and scratchiness of Vitaphone. He put a line of young men through their regular drill, his rapped instructions, the crunch of the gravel and the slapping of hands on rifles, all perfectly captured. Far

63

away in the background, passing automobiles emitted only the faintest hum. Best of all, the sound did not have the shattering unevenness of Vitaphone shorts. Even when the West Point Academy Band brassily went through its paces in a rendition of Sousa marches, the sound was tolerable and even pleasant. Smiling at the newsmen's responses, Fox told them: "In five years the silent picture will be no longer silent. The players will have to undergo courses in elocution to prepare themselves for talking photoplays."

But Fox's greatest triumph came a few weeks later, on May 21. That day the nation had gone "Lindy crazy." Among the contenders for the hotelier Raymond Orteig's $25,000 price for the first flyer to span the Atlantic from New York to Paris, was Charles A. Lindbergh. Personifying American youth at its most frank, honest, open, clean-cut and courageous, Lindbergh decided to fly his gray monoplane, *The Spirit of St. Louis,* from Roosevelt Field, Long Island, in rain and fog on the morning of May 20. Several hundred people braved the cold of the night air, as Lindbergh slept, rising shortly after 2:00 AM to prepare for the aerial odyssey. The crowd went wild with excitement as Lindy, dressed in his famous fur-lined flying suit, warmed up the motor, fought with it as it choked in the icy air, then smiled broadly as *The Spirit* hurtled off the ground, only to plunge into mud minutes later. Bumping, leapfrogging and slapping through churned up earth, missing a tractor by only a few feet and dangerously skimming over a sudden fall of soil, *The Spirit of St. Louis* at last began its bucking, jolting journey over the tension wires into a patch of blue sky on its way to Paris.

On May 20, the biggest boxing match of the season— between Moloney and Sharkey at the Yankee Stadium— featured a moment of highly charged emotion when the match commentator called on the 40,000 people to bare their heads to pray for Lindy.

On May 21 when Lindbergh was reported to have

safely reached the end of his journey, an overwhelming wave of mass hysteria engulfed America. And it was at that precise psychological moment, when the public was at its most frenzied and its most vulnerable, that Fox chose to strike with his new invention.

For he had achieved a masterstroke of showmanship: he had seen to it that his determined little team of newsreel-makers had been present with recorders at Roosevelt Field. All over New York he splashed the announcement that on the night of Lindy's arrival in Paris he would show films of the takeoff. The Roxy, naturally, was packed that night, but no one was prepared for the moment that was to come.

The instant the first shots of the rainswept field were flashed onto the screen, the audience was astonished to hear a spluttering, coughing sound boomed out of every loudspeaker in the giant theatre. It was the sound of Lindy's motor! When the 6000 people could not only see but hear Lindy's departure, they stood and cheered Movietone resoundingly. Nothing on the first night of *Don Juan* had begun to equal this.

Fox wasted no time in building on this foundation: he charted Lindy's triumphal progress as he returned home, brought by cruiser, welcomed at a presidential open-air festivity, paraded through Washington followed by a truck containing 55,000 telegrams, and through New York under a blizzard made of 1800 tons of tickertape.

As a direct answer to Fox's venture, Jack Warner increased production of the Vitaphone shorts. He put in charge of them Bryan Foy, a former vaudevillean and the son of Eddie Foy, Senior.

In late 1926 Bryan Foy began making a series at the Sunset Boulevard studios, to which all the equipment from the Brooklyn studio was transferred.* His first short

---

* During 1926–1939 Foy made a total of 600 shorts at the rate of two a week, working every day including Sunday. Among his stars were Beatrice Lillie and Gertrude Lawrence.

was entitled *The Pullman Porters*. It lasted exactly nine minutes in order to coincide exactly with a pre-recorded disc. The singing actors had to move along a set of a train corridor and compartments, and sometimes the vibration of their feet or voices jolted the needles off the discs, necessitating a complete retake. Foy had to throw his voice in imitation of a particular player whose voice was too far from a planted microphone.

For a short entitled *French Leave,* Foy showed soldiers in the trenches, playing hookey and carousing in an inn; finally, they were marched off to jail by military police. Foy had the studio art department build three sets alongside each other: the trenches, the inn, the jail. When one scene was finished, the lights were dimmed and the actors, invisible to the audience in the darkness, dodged onto the next set, and so on until the reel was over.

Much of Foy's work involved a simple recapitulation of vaudeville acts, shot by Eddie DuPar, without any significant movement within the frame. He kept churning out two a week; but there was a problem in marketing the shorts at first as very few theatres were wired for sound.

While Foy proceeded with these shorts, the Warners decided to use some talking and singing sequences in their previously bought property, *The Jazz Singer,* obtained grudgingly after Charles Van Enger's original suggestion. Samson Raphaelson's sentimental play about Jewish life in New York appealed to the Jewish company of Goldman, Sachs, which had advanced a substantial sum to acquire the rights. George Jessel had appeared in the production with great success on the stage. Originally, it had been intended to star George Jessel in the silent version. But when Jessel spoke to Eddie Cantor, his very close friend, about playing the part, Cantor advised him to insist on doubling the fee offered in view of the fact that songs were to be added. The brothers were not prepared to increase the sum. However, George Jessel claims today that the company had paid him five useless checks in a row for his work on the vaudeville shorts made by Sam Warner and Eddie DuPar in New York. In the meantime Sam Warner had the idea of signing Al Jolson to make the picture. Without the knowledge of the other members of the family, he sent Morris Safier of the New York office to Denver, Colorado, where Jolson was touring in the production.

At this time, Bryan Foy was making a test of William (Buster) Collier as a possible alternative to Jessel. A special room—15 feet by 30 feet—was built of heavy brick, with a very large window through which the cumbersome talkie camera could shoot. Jack Warner told Collier, who couldn't sing, to deliver a song—"anything"—and that if he did this successfully, he might be able to play in *The Jazz Singer*. Policemen with whistles were stationed on Sunset Boulevard outside, surrounding the entire block, and at a given signal from Jack Warner they all blew their whistles at once. Traffic stopped in the street; nobody inside the studio must utter a word on pain of instant dismissal, and from eight o'clock at night until 4:00 AM Collier kept singing over and over again, anything that came into his head, while the camera crew groaned at the sound of his voice. Meanwhile, Jack Warner had neglected to note one detail: there was virtually no ventilation at all in the camera booth, so that at the end of a take, the door burst open and the three cameramen inside tumbled out in a heap, gasping for breath.

Meanwhile, Sam Warner and Morris Safier of the New York office were talking with Jolson in Detroit. Jolson was perfectly confident in asking for a large piece of Warner stock, and for $75,000, one third in cash and the rest in weekly instalments of $6250 a week, part of these sums being reinvested in the picture so as to earn him a percentage of its profits. The agreement was dependent upon Jolson's first tests in Hollywood being entirely satisfactory. They were, and the arrangement went ahead.

He earned every cent of it. Shooting *The Jazz Singer*

under the direction of Alan Crosland was fast and tough, reminding Jolson that he had good reason for backing out of an earlier film project, D. W. Griffith's *Mamma's Boy*. Making the sound portions of the film after it was finished silent caused Jolson and the director Alan Crosland agonizing problems. As always, once 1000 feet of film at a time had been synchronized with the giant discs it could never be cut or tampered with again because the voices would not match with the lip movements. Songs were Vitaphoned at different points. In the action, every part of a reel which did not offer songs was filmed first. Then the reel was edited, and titles added. The singing scenes were rehearsed continuously until they were perfect, with Sam Warner in charge. They had to be timed to a split second before pre-recording, because the slightest variance could be fatal to the film.

Blank film was fitted into the developed non-speaking footage, cut to exactly the same length that dialogue would take. Four microphone circuits were wired up. One was for the orchestra and one each for the sets built side-by-side and representing the different rooms where Jolson would sing the songs. All the sets had to be lit and dressed with different players and soundproof cameras ready to grind.

First, the unfinished reel was flashed onto a screen in front of the orchestra. When the blank feet of film began they started to play a medley of Tchaikovsky, Grieg, Brahms, and Jewish themes. At that precise moment, Jolson, also on the first set, started to talk, and his words were conveyed to the same disc while the camera recorded his actions. The instant the dialogue was over he went to the next sound stage, with a lightning change in between, while the orchestra watched the intervening feet until the next blank space appeared and a light cue told him he must start to speak. Then he moved to the third set.

Since nothing could be repeated, Jolson—an incorrigible practical joker—decided to ad lib a few lines in his traditional stage manner for the screen. Alan Crosland and the technicians were dismayed when he rattled off some stray words, since they had no intention of using recorded dialogue, and had no idea whether what he said would make sense. But his ad libs, including the famous, "Hey, ma, listen to this!" and "Wait a minute, wait a minute, you ain't heard nothing yet!" were inexorably recorded, and so was a long extraordinary address to his mother, played by Eugenie Besserer, telling her she can look forward to wearing a splendid wardrobe, travelling to Coney Island, and occupying a comfortable home in the Bronx.

Hal Mohr, the cameraman, was faced with a peculiar problem that had a very funny result. Because arc lamps, the large, glowing lights that were used to light movie sets at the time, would fizz noisily and be heard on the discs, he had to use incandescent lights for the sound film scenes. The new panchromatic film which had come in only 18 months earlier, lent itself ideally to incandescent lighting, providing that enormous banks of incandescents were used. For the silent scenes, arcs and orthochromatic film were used as usual.

May McAvoy, the female star opposite Jolson, had bright red hair. On orthochromatic film it came out black; on panchromatic it came out white. Therefore, as May McAvoy moved from a silent scene into a sound one, her hair changed color; she would walk out of one room brunette, and enter another blonde.

Amusingly also, during one silent scene the sound technicians were horrified to hear a slow, insistent creaking sound. After searching every inch of the stage, they were embarrassed to discover that the source of the creaking was Mrs. Ben Warner, who was watching the shooting from an old rocking chair. Gently but firmly, the matriarch of the clan was removed, together with her chair, from the set for the remainder of the shooting.

The Jazz Singer opened at the Warner Theater in New

York on October 7, 1927, before a brilliant society audience. The film opened with a vivid evocation of Brooklyn streets, beautifully shot by Hal Mohr with concealed, truck-borne cameras on location in New York, accompanied by the Vitaphone players vigorously rendering "East Side, West Side." In a bar, the 13-year-old Jewish boy Jakie Rabinowitz (played by Bobby Gordon) was introduced with a brief title, and the audience tensed as he opened his mouth and started to sing. It was a tremendous moment: the words of "My Gal Sal" ("They called her frivolous Sal, a peculiar sort of a gal"), sung expertly in Gordon's very true, strong voice, had the audience on its feet cheering and whistling. But the real excitement was still to come.

As Hal Mohr focuses on Coffee Dan's after-theatre cafe in San Francisco, and the Vitaphone violinists and bass players render a jazz theme, Jakie (Al Jolson) now grown up, threads his way through the tables, and a title says: "Wish me luck!" He is speaking to his friend, played by William Demarest. He is about to make his singing debut. "Wonderful Pals," the next title says, "are hard to find." And a moment later he breaks triumphantly into "Dirty Hands, Dirty Face!"

As the audience at the Warner Theater went wild, Jolson followed the song with the immortal words ad-libbed in Hollywood to the astonishment of Mohr and Alan Crosland: the first spoken words ever uttered in an American motion picture: "Wait a minute, wait a minute! You ain't heard nothing yet! Wait a minute I tell ya, you ain't heard nothing. You want to hear 'Toot, Toot, Tootsie'? All right, hold on. [To the pianist] Louis, listen! Play 'Toot, Toot, Tootsie' three/four if you understand. In the third chorus I whistle. Now give it to them hard and heavy. Go right ahead!" And still in an hysterical state of excitement, Jolson sang "Tootsie" with everything he had.

No one who ever attended that premiere would ever

forget the moment, and the audience was right up there identifying with the clients at Coffee Dan's as they rattled their cups and hammered the tables. Later in the picture, Jolson again broke into dialogue, in an ecstatically ad-libbed conversation with his mother as he vamped the music at the piano in her shabby little room, telling her what would happen when he was rich and successful:

"Do you like that mother? I'll play another. I'd rather please you than anybody I know. Oh darling, will you give me something? You'll never guess! [a kiss]. Shut your eyes mamma! Shut them for your little Jakie! Oh, I'm going to steal something! I'll give it back to you! Someday . . . you'll see if I don't! Mamma darling, if I'm a success on the show well, we're going to move from here. We are going to move up to the Bronx. A lot of nice green grass up there . . .

"And a whole lot of people you know: the Ginsbergs, the Guttenbergs, and the Goldbergs and a whole lot of Bergs. I don't know 'em all. I'm going to buy you a nice black silk dress, mamma. You'll see Mrs. Friedman, the butcher's wife. She'll be jealous of you. Oh yes, you'll see if she isn't. I'm going to get you a nice pink dress to go with your brown eyes . . . what do you mean no? Yes you'll wear pink—*or else* you'll wear pink! Oh, darling, oh, I'm going to take you to Coney Island, oh yes, we'll ride over 'Shoot the Chutes,' and you know 'The Dark Mill'? Have you ever been in 'The Dark Mill'? With me it's all right. I'll kiss you and hug you, you'll see if I don't!"

That, followed by "Mother of Mine," "Blue Skies," the "Kol Nidre" and a dynamic rendition of "Mammy," sung from a replica of the Winter Garden stage, brought the audience to an unequalled pitch of hysteria. They cheered and cheered and refused to sit down. William Demarest felt a shiver run along his spine like the one he felt when he heard the *Titanic* had gone down. The banker Otto Kahn turned to his wife and said, "You and I will never see a moment like this again."

Al Jolson wept in a stage box. Irving Berlin was unable to contain his tears. The Kodak King Jules Brulatour squeezed his good friend Hope Hampton's hand very tight. It was a moment no one present felt they would ever forget; it was a moment none of them still living has forgotten. They talk of it today with awe, because in 1927 it was as though men had landed on the moon. The shaky, abrasive voice of the movies had been heard for the first time. Talkies had been born.

6

A New Era

DURING THE SHOOTING OF
The Jazz Singer, Sam Warner had fallen seriously ill in
Los Angeles. The origin of the illness could be traced
back several years: he had thrown a motorcycle-riding
stunt man, Slim Cole, out of the studio; the man had returned later in the day and tussled with him, punching
him on the nose and breaking it permanently. Small,
splintered pieces of bone at the back of the nose were not
operated on, and worked their way into the antrum, setting up a serious infection which finally became dangerous. Sam underwent a series of six operations, but the antrum had been very severely inflamed. On October 1, he
was admitted to the Lutheran Hospital where Dr. George
McCoy tried to save his life. He began to sink on the
night of October 4, and at 3:17 in the morning of October
5, he slipped into his final sleep.

As soon as they received word, Harry, Albert and Jack, all of whom were in New York, took the train to Los Angeles, missing *The Jazz Singer*'s New York premiere. When they reached Arizona, another cable informed them that Sam only had a very few hours to live. Even in those early days of air travel, they tried to charter a plane, without success.

On October 9, the funeral services were held at Bresee Brothers on Washington Boulevard, simultaneously with a service at Warner Brothers itself. Among the honorary pallbearers were Motley Flint, Harry Rapf, Darryl Zanuck, Bryan Foy, Hal Wallis, Cecil B. DeMille, Mack Sennett, Adolphe Menjou, Lubitsch, George Groves, Sol Lesser, Sid Grauman, and Alan Crosland. At the family service, Rabbi Magnin spoke of Sam's "worthy family life and his kindness to parents and friends as well as his success in the business world."

At the studio service, the Rev. Neal Dodd officiated and Edward Davis, a friend of Sam's, spoke of his accomplishments. At Bresee Brothers, the Jewish ritual was given in full; at the studio, Parrish Williams sang "Yohrzeit" and the "Kol Nidre." *

In 1926, Warners had declared a loss to shareholders of over $100,000, and that figure merely hinted at the extent of their misfortune. In 1927, Motley Flint began to disentangle himself from the investment banking business, leaving the company virtually dependent on Goldman, Sachs in New York. In 1927, they barely scraped through, just managing to achieve profits of some $16,500. But the gamble with *The Jazz Singer* began to pay off al-

---

* The brothers were very concerned about the welfare of Sam's eight-month-old daughter, Lita. She was the child of Sam and Lina Basquette. The brothers felt that Mrs. Warner was an unfit mother and after a bitter custody battle the child was officially adopted by Harry.

most at once. More and more theatres were wired for sound, while Western Electric boosted its installation charges from $5000 to $25,000 a theatre. In order to equip their own theatres, the Warners had to borrow from their own private companies (particularly Harry Warner's Renraw) but fortunately the receipts at the box office were substantial enough to justify the risk.

On January 26, 1928, the brothers announced that all pictures made that year would have Vitaphone sequences. During the brothers' absence in the East and in Europe, Bryan Foy, in February, took the law into his own hands and extended two shorts into a full-length all-talking feature, *The Lights of New York*, with Cullen Landis, and Helene Costello. The sound track was a cacophony of street noises, recorded in special trucks which were driven through downtown Los Angeles. The story was a lame account of underworld life, and the direction extremely rudimentary: the characters were seen crouching around table lamps, large cigarette boxes, or pen and ink stands, all of which concealed microphones. The result was a motion picture that resembled nothing so much as a photographed radio play.

During the filming, lights were in such short supply that car headlamps were often used or powerful 10K lights that burned the players' faces, provoking the grim contemporary jokes, "Don't wear a celluloid collar, or you'll have a necklace of fire," and "if you want to light a cigar, you can do it off the actor's skin." Ingenious synchronizing devices supposed to ensure that the cameras were in constant accord with the recording apparatus often went awry when players wandered beyond the microphone's range and a shout became a whisper. Often they looked painfully self-conscious in the rushes, all too obviously kept anxious eyes fixed on the microphone positions. Rehearsals were interminable; when shooting finally started a whistle blew and the great steel doors, barring every external sound, slammed shut, creating temperatures that ranged up to 100 degrees and beyond.

When a take ended, a two blast whistle indicated that everyone could relax—more or less. Sometimes as many as 15 records were ruined, at enormous cost, because a hammer was dropped or someone tripped over a wire during a scene. Later came a tormenting inquest: the listening booth, resembling a traffic tower and looming above the stage, disgorged a feverish little group of men who told the director exactly what was wrong with a sequence.

Absolute secrecy surrounded the amplifying and recording rooms. Reporters were forbidden to enter them, or even to describe what they saw during shooting. Official visitors were rigorously excluded—no matter if they were visiting heads of state. Every step of the way, a publicity man followed a few writers who managed to penetrate the Warner fastness, insisting maddeningly on supervising every note made.

The sound-stage atmosphere was suffocatingly sinister and strange: the great cameras in threes or fours like wheeled gray tanks with peering cold eyes gliding in on the players, microphone wires hung in stretched gleaming cobwebs above their heads, the director making dumb-show signals, the actors feeling like blind men for the microphone leads, and the slightest sneeze or cough resulting in screaming directorial rages, near hysterics among the sound recorders who ruled the directors with an iron hand, and yet another painful retake as the great wax discs whirred imperviously on.

The Lights of New York was an immediate success, and by mid-1928, the studio had been virtually refitted for sound: Rin-Tin-Tin was heard as well as seen, barking vigorously in a new feature, *Land of the Silver Fox*, being shot at Truckee. That spring, the Warners rushed out silent films with additional talking sequences: *Tenderloin*, directed by Michael Curtiz, and *Glorious Betsy*, directed by Alan Crosland. Though both films made money because of their novel techniques, they were not warmly received by the critics or the public.

Michael Curtiz' *Tenderloin,* described as "the first of the speaking shadow stories," was an underworld melodrama: Dolores Costello played a New York East Side cafe dancer who, while walking home exhausted one night, sees someone throw a bag over a fence; it contains money stolen from a bank, tossed away because the thieves are surprised in a raid. The girl is seized by police and questioned, but the bag at the time of her arrest has been filled with wastepaper and brass slugs. The rest of the film deals with the question: was she implicated in the robbery, and if not, who hid the money? Conrad Nagel played a handsome crook who befriended and finally became the lover of the suspected dancer.

Premiered in New York, the film, with the stars' voices uncomfortably distorted and "tubby," earned laughter and boos from the first night audience. Alan Crosland's *Glorious Betsy,* also starring Costello and Nagel, suffered from an equally calamitous public and critical reaction. Nagel, as Jerome Bonaparte, in a story of Jerome's love affair with an American girl, Betsy Patterson, spoke with a broad American accent, and in one scene when whispers were called for, his voice echoed deafeningly through the auditorium. The kissing scenes were so loud that every time Nagel's and Costello's lips met it was like a clapping of hands. The audience did not clap. When at the New York premiere Dolores Costello uttered the last line in the picture, "My tomorrow has come," a wag in the stalls yelled out, "Thank the good Lord for that!"

Unofficially, and later officially, the up-and-coming Darryl F. Zanuck became head of production, replacing the unfortunate young Bennie Ziedman, who was pushed out in a power play. On July 21, Warners began work on its fourth sound stage, which cost $200,000 and measured

200 by 300 feet. That same month it was announced that the bond issue floated when the studio was at its lowest ebb, would be repaid in full, and that Vitaphone had now been installed in more than 400 theatres. Meanwhile, the Warners had made another "speaking shadow story," *The Lion and the Mouse,* with Lionel Barrymore and May McAvoy.

In the same year, Lloyd Bacon directed Al Jolson in *The Singing Fool,* a successor to *The Jazz Singer* that was just as sentimental as its predecessor. After *The Singing Fool* Jack Warner and Darryl F. Zanuck took a bold step and starred Fannie Brice in a story specially written for her, and based in part on her life, *My Man.* The film was skillfully directed by Archie Mayo and written by Robert Lord; in it, Miss Brice sang her famous hits "My Man," * by Channing Pollock and Maurice Yvain, "Second-Hand Rose," by Grant Clarke and James Hanley, "I'd Rather Be Blue," by Billy Rose and Fred Fisher, among other songs. It was a simple, unaffected story, about Fanny Brand who works for a theatrical costumer and falls in love with an elastic exerciser demonstrator, Joe Halsey (played by Guinn Williams). Fanny manages to achieve a stage career with the aid of a Ziegfeld-like producer, Landau (Andre de Segurola), and she defeats the machinations of her sister Edna Brand in order to secure Joe's hand in marriage.

The most bizarre of the new talkies made in 1928 was *The Terror,* directed by Roy Del Ruth, starring May McAvoy, Louise Fazenda, and Edward Everett Horton. Based on an Edgar Wallace novel, it was the story of an insane killer who lives in an old British inn. He terrorizes the guests, particularly with some eerie organ recitals, before he is exposed after a night of horror.

* The title had been used for a Vitagraph Company of America production of 1924, starring Patsy Ruth Miller, and with an entirely different story.

The film was introduced by Conrad Nagel, in a long cloak, speaking the titles. Among the sound effects were heavy rain, thunder and lightning, the high-pitched whine of an organ in a wind, and the sudden creak of a floorboard as the villain emerges to terrify the heroine. Unfortunately, the film was not a success in England: audiences in London laughed uncontrollably when May McAvoy said plaintively and squeakily in her American accent, "Daddy, can you hear the organ?" But in the United States it was very successful indeed.

Two remarkable films were made by Warners in the period without talkie sound tracks, but with musical accompaniment and sound effects only: Alan Crosland's *In Old San Francisco*, and Michael Curtiz' *Noah's Ark*. *In Old San Francisco* was chiefly notable for its authentic recreation of the San Francisco earthquake, which the cameraman, Hal Mohr, had actually experienced as a child. Balsa wood sets were used which could fall on the characters without injury; but the shots of the shaking buildings were achieved by means of an amazing camera trick which Mohr devised. He took a square reducing glass that had optics sufficient to widen the angle, and mounted it in a wooden frame supported by a rubbery substance that allowed it to float freely within the frame. The frame was mounted on the front unit arm of the camera. Mohr lined the shots up through the framed lens, tapping the framework gently; this caused the lens to jiggle and distort the image so that the entire miniature set of the city seemed to wobble.

For *Noah's Ark*, Mohr again supplied a rich visual surface, decorating the resplendent sets of Anton Grot built at the Vitagraph Studios. The most difficult scenes to be shot were those of the flooding of the great city, with seemingly every stunt man in Hollywood engaged to play the very dangerous scenes. The set of a temple was supposed to collapse on 450 people, making one of the most extraordinary shots in the history of the motion picture. Mohr was horrified to discover upon examining the scene in advance for lighting purposes that no shots would be faked, and the plaster walls would in fact engulf not only the stunt men, but ordinary extras as well.

Mohr resigned at once, and was replaced by Barney McGill and William Rees. The picture went ahead, and the scene of the collapse of the temple caused several broken legs, and—according to some reports—two deaths.

Ever since the brothers' onslaught on the Big Three, they had been determined to take over First National, whose chief, Al Rockett, had been particularly opposed to their criticisms. They knew that the Stanley Company of America, a massive theatre owning combine, centered in Philadelphia, and the Fox Film Corporation, owned between them a controlling interest in First National. In the first place, Harry Warner, backed and abetted by Waddill Catchings of Goldman, Sachs, persuaded William Fox to sell his 29% interest in the company, while Waddill Catchings bought a large slice of Stanley and arranged a place on its board. Piece by piece, Catchings and Harry Warner bought up the Stanley corporation, solving the company's major problem of having sufficient theatres in which to exhibit Vitaphone. On September 13, Warners acquired complete control of the Stanley corporation for $100 million; and almost at once Warner stock, selling at $28 the previous year, rose to an extraordinary $130 a share. On September 27, Warners bought an additional 19,000 shares of First National, bringing its holdings to 42,000 of a total of 75,000 shares. On September 30, it was announced that Irving Rossheim, former president of Stanley, would now be president of First National. By October 11, the situation had settled down: Warners would move into the First National studio at Burbank; Jack

Warner would be in complete charge of production at the studio, with Darryl F. Zanuck directly under him. Al Rockett would remain production chief of the First National outfit; William Koenig would be in charge of the Warner end of the business, Robert North of the First National end. Both companies would work side by side, sharing Vitaphone facilities. The bullish feelings of the Warners were confirmed in a release to the press dated November 9, 1928, that their net income for the year was $2,044,841, or $3.72 a share. By late November, negotiations were complete for the purchase of the Skouras Brothers theatres of St. Louis, and every bank loan was finally paid off. And a small item in the press, destined to be highly significant, was that Hal B. Wallis, in charge of publicity at Warners, would be promoted to studio manager of First National.

At the outset of 1929, the Warners profits had climbed to just under three million dollars net. There was talk, quickly quashed by the brothers, of a merger with Metro-Goldwyn-Mayer; by March, financial reporters on both coasts were printing speculative articles on an immense merger of Warners and Fox which would involve a complete takeover of the Loew's theatre chain, which in turn owned M-G-M. On March 29, Joe Schenck, vice-president and chairman of the board of United Artists, announced that it was quite probable United Artists would sell 50 percent of its entire common stock to Warners.

What all this meant was that the brothers, exhilarated by the great success of the preceding months, were seeking to blend in and perhaps absorb virtually all of the hated "Big Three." With First National under their collective belt, they wanted M-G-M and United Artists as well. Charlie Chaplin—a director of United Artists—vigorously opposed the merger, seeking a complete independence of the company which he had helped to found.

Meanwhile, the Warners were claiming damages in New York from Electrical Research Products, Inc., which had patented the Vitagraph process (ERPI, as it was known, was a subsidiary of Western Electric), for not having paid a royalty on releasing the equipment to other companies. By early 1930, the complicated problems were sorted out: virtually all of the Hollywood companies used sound-on-film, perfected by Western Electric/ERPI, and Warners changed to sound-on-film the moment its quality equalled that of sound-on-disc.

The merger with United Artists was finally called off in June, but Warners continued to expand as an independent entity. In July, they leased the historic Lasky ranch in the San Fernando Valley, scene of the making of many early Cecil B. DeMille films, including *The Rose of the Rancho*. In August they bought (through a new corporation, the Warner Brothers Downtown Theatres) the Pantages Theatres in Los Angeles and Fresno. In November, yet another merger, never consummated, was being seriously discussed between Warners and Paramount. And they began building a new theatre between Cahuenga and Wilcox Boulevards in Hollywood, with a capacity of 3500 and a handsome Moroccan decor.

At the end of 1929, just before the Wall Street crash, the company enjoyed profits of 16 million dollars. The crash affected the shares only slightly; and they recovered immediately after it was over. By the outset of 1930, Warners owned some 25% of the nation's theatres, and announced that they would begin the new year with the first "original operetta written for the screen," *Viennese Nights*.

Heel Taps
and Gunshots

Nineteen twenty-nine
and 1930 were years of consolidation for the booming
company and its associate First National. Jack Warner and
Darryl Zanuck jointly launched a policy of all-talking musicals, including *The Desert Song*, which was released in
April, 1929: it starred John Boles, a baseball southpaw
from Texas, and Carlotta King, whom Jack Warner signed
after hearing her sing "If One Flower Grows Alone" on
radio. Equally important was *Gold-Diggers of Broadway*,
based on the title and not the story of Belasco's *The Gold
Diggers*, which had been filmed with Hope Hampton in
1923. *Gold-Diggers of Broadway* was notable for being
the first "all-color, all dialog" musical. It starred Winnie
Lightner, a raucous comedienne who had graduated after
years as a part of "Newton Alexander and the Lightner

Sisters" from the hard school of vaudeville; she had appeared in two of the earliest vaudeville shorts made at the Vitagraph studios in New York, and Jack Warner had admired the uninhibited vulgarity of her style. She flung herself with great enthusiasm into the production, despite shooting schedules which ran 18 hours at a stretch, and heat so intense from the arclights used for color filming that the players' hair smoked. Nick Lucas played admirably opposite her, and Nancy Welford and Conway Tearle provided excellent foils.

The two most elaborate Warner musicals of 1929 were *On with the Show* and *The Show of Shows*, theatrical revues with remarkably few concessions to cinematic techniques of presentation. The star of *On with the Show* was Betty Compson, wife of the director James Cruze, who had distinguished himself at Paramount with such celebrated films as *The Covered Wagon* and *Old Ironsides*. When Warners merged with First National Miss Compson was absorbed; she had begun work on a film called *The Barker*, which was remade as a part-talkie. She recorded well, and despite the fact that she could neither sing nor dance, Zanuck cast her in *On with the Show* as a star of the musical stage. A professional dancer took her place in long shots, and a professional singer pre-recorded her voice while she mouthed silently at the camera.

The musical "wave" proved to be short-lived; the public was quickly bored and saturated by these films and wanted something new. Zanuck was impatient following the very bad reception for Ray Enright's *Golden Dawn*, a preposterous operetta by Oscar Hammerstein II, Otto Harbach, Emmerich Kalman and Herbert Stothart, about a girl (played by Vivienne Segal) who is captured by an African tribe and its sadistic chieftain, acted by Noah Beery in blackface. The sequence in which Miss Segal was betrothed to an African idol, Mulunghu, was particularly absurd; and Noah Beery's "Whip Song," with its extraordinary sado-masochistic lyrics, was the nadir of bad taste. The film was laughed off the screen. There could be no question that the time had come for a new mode, and early in 1930 Jack Warner and Zanuck began urgently seeking new ideas.

In those same weeks the company's finances began to look a little shaky. The enormous enthusiasm of the brothers had evidently carried them too far. Business began to decline sharply, and it was evident that the novelty not only of musicals but of talkies as a whole had already worn off. There was no dividend in the last quarter of 1930 and stockholders were asked to buy one new share at $20 for each single share held. Goldman, Sachs and Hayden Stone and Co. arranged for 755,000 new shares to be issued, providing an urgently needed $17 million dollars in fresh capital. Various shareholders, led by a severely disaffected Boston businessman, Ira Nelson, filed a petition with the Court of Chancery in Wilmington, Delaware, asking for the appointment of a receiver in bankruptcy for Warner Brothers Pictures, charging mismanagement: Nelson claimed the brothers were deliberately depreciating the value of their stock. The receivership charge was dismissed by Chief Justice Penniwill of Delaware on the grounds that the bill as filed was neither signed nor verified by the complainant as called for by Rule 31 of the court.

On November 21, 1930, the executive offices and cutting rooms of Warner Brothers were moved to the First National studios at Burbank, while pictures continued to be made at the Sunset studio and at Vitagraph. Zanuck and Jack Warner jointly decided that the policy of making musicals must at once be replaced. Zanuck decided on a "headline news" policy, in which the studio would focus on crime and corruption in American society, in stories drawn from the newspaper headlines. It was this policy which carried the company through the very rocky period which lay immediately ahead.

Meanwhile, an unsettling event occurred to interrupt the enthusiasm of the Warners during 1930. On July 31, the Caddo Company, Inc., headed by Howard Hughes, filed suit in the United States District Court in New York against Warner Brothers, Inc. and First National Pictures, charging that the larger part of the film *The Dawn Patrol*, directed by Howard Hawks, and written by a former flyer, John Monk Saunders, had been stolen from Hughes' film *Hell's Angels*. The complaint, which called for a complete withdrawal of *The Dawn Patrol* from all theatres, asserted that a writer named Robert Mackay in 1922 had written a story called *Somewhere in Mexico*, which he had sold to the director Marshall Neilan in 1927. Neilan and Benjamin Glazer had adapted the story and entitled it *Hell's Angels*, which, the plaintiffs claimed, had been lifted bodily and placed into the screenplay of *The Dawn Patrol*. Next day, Gainsborough Pictures of Great Britain, Welsh, Pearson and Elder, lawyers, and the writer R. C. Sherriff sued Warners for using substantial portions of Sherriff's play *Journey's End*, currently prepared for the screen at Universal, in the same film. On August 6, United States District Judge Cosgrove screened all three films at First National studios to determine whether a temporary injunction against screenings of *The Dawn Patrol* should be issued. He decided that the comparisons between the three films simply proved that similar events of the war had been drawn from, and *The Dawn Patrol* was permitted to circulate.

A most severe shock in July was the sudden death of Motley Flint. Although Flint had begun to drift away from the company, and had suffered a number of reverses—he had been accused of involvement in the Julian Petroleum scandal, in which a number of leading businessmen were charged with usury, and had resigned his position with the Security Bank—he had remained very close to the brothers. On Monday morning, July 14, 1930, Flint was giving testimony in Superior Judge Collier's court in downtown Los Angeles in the matter of David O. Selznick's suit against the Security-First National Bank for recovery of an unreturned sum of $250,000. As Flint stepped off the witness stand, he passed by the counsel table and through a narrow wooden gate in the railing which separated the spectators' section from the courtroom proper. He stopped to speak for a moment to David O. Selznick's mother, Mrs. Lewis Selznick; at that moment a man jumped forward from a seat just behind Mrs. Selznick, rested a gun on her shoulder and fired at Flint, shooting him through the neck and chest. Flint fell to the floor, dying instantly. Judge Collier ran over to the killer, who had sunk back into his seat, and demanded the gun. The murderer was arrested at once and identified as Frank Keaton, a real estate man who had lost $50,000 in investments in Flint's various interests.*

Only six months later, in February, 1931, the brothers suffered yet another grief: the handsome and athletic Lewis Warner, the 22-year-old eldest son of Harry, fell ill in Havana, Cuba, from an infected wisdom tooth. Albert and Harry rushed to his bedside, together with Dr. Thomas J. Unger, medical adviser to the studio; and Lewis was transferred by chartered plane to Miami and then by special ambulance and private railroad car to New York. Unfortunately, septic poisoning had set in, and Lewis was stricken with double pneumonia shortly after admission to The Doctor's Hospital on East End Avenue and 87th Street. He died, after a gallant struggle, on April 5.

These grievous shocks occurred during a time of fran-

---

* Because of some doubt of his sanity, Keaton escaped hanging (then the method of execution in California) and served prison terms of more than 25 years.

tic activity by the Warners. A remorseless devotion to factory or San Quentin duty, to "God, country and Yale," was the policy which forged the major studio Warners became in the wake of the "gimmick" of talkies. The motivation in the minds of the employees was not necessarily a devotion to art, but rather the determination to sustain a high standard of living in time of want. Cars, large houses, huge insurance programs, servants, all must be sustained. Expensive divorces had to be paid for, children put through high school. It was all a championship game that had to be played, and there was the constant sense of pressure to make a film better than those being made at Paramount or M-G-M.

In that harsh period, the publicity department constantly tried to give the impression that Warners was just a big, happy family, with everybody working together harmoniously; and today a number of distinguished alumni of the studio still seek to give that impression. Actually, it was a period of pressure, constant work (on Saturdays, everyone toiled through the night, returning home on Sunday as the sun hit the pillows) and quarrelling, an existence relieved only by the comparatively high salaries during the Depression, and the harsh gallows humor or "jokes on the warden," which animated the conversation of the crews ("If you joined the Foreign Legion to get away from Warners, you deserved a medal for courage" was one common line, bandied frequently in the commissary).

The stock company was established quickly: George Arliss, Cagney, Robinson, Blondell, and, later, Kay Francis, Bette Davis, Ann Dvorak, Bogart: these people, and dozens more, were put on the payroll like bank clerks, given strictly limited vacations—which could be cancelled at a moment's notice—and put on suspension or even dismissed without recompense if they refused to play the roles to which they were assigned. The corps of producers and writers had strict instructions from Jack

Warner to make sure that absolutely nobody was ever left idle for a moment. If no vehicle was fully prepared for a star, Jack Warner and Darryl Zanuck were to be seen pacing uneasily about, chewing hard on their expensive cigars.

Sometimes the pressure was so severe that the various scenarists would sit on the set with typewriters; when they were finished with a page, a second assistant would pull it out of the machine and hand it to the director. Vinegary and peppery, Zanuck was constantly on the scene changing everything. In the office, too, he was deeply involved in arguments and discussions on the writing, sessions the director attended also.

More out of necessity than out of crusading zeal, Warners gradually assumed, in 1931, an atmosphere resembling that of the city room of a leading New York tabloid newspaper. Zanuck saw to it that the policy for writers, directors and players was clearly set down: the opening shots must plunge the audience into a world of violence, tension and big city excitement, making a first reel the equivalent of a first paragraph in a front page story. Mingling sentiment, melodrama and comedy, the story must progress without a slow moment, each scene taken at a high point, the progression swift, until a knockout denouement. The actors and actresses must deliver their lines with the rapidity and ferocity of machine-gun bullets. America was in the midst of a depression, in the midst of a wave of crime; very well then, Warners would be the studio which commented, vigorously and fearlessly, on the sources of the evil in society. M-G-M could provide escapism, Paramount its shimmering romantic comedies, Universal its horror films, but Warners would be the studio of the people, for the people. It was a gimmick which worked, but the financial problems went on and on.

First and most famous of the gangster films, *Little Caesar* was made under the First National imprint in 1930, and released in 1931. W. R. Burnett brought his famous book to the studio story department, and Jack Warner read it. Mervyn LeRoy heard about it and immediately sat up all night reading the book. Warner agreed at once to his directing it, and they jointly approached Edward G. Robinson to play the leading role. Darryl F. Zanuck was in charge of the production, with Hal Wallis as producer; the film confirmed the position of all three men as among the most gifted picture makers in Hollywood.

It is true that today *Little Caesar* seems stiff and awkward, some of the acting uncomfortable and microphone-conscious. But in the context of its period the production was in every way extraordinary. At the height of Al Capone's power, it daringly caricatured him as a conceited, arrogant Italian gangster, infantile in his self-admiration, ruthless in the mowing down of friend and enemy alike. And in the title role of Rico Bandello the Warners offered a man of very superior talent. Edward G. Robinson had suffered from a halting career in movies following his extraordinary performance as Scarsi in the Broadway stage production of *The Racket*. Squat, runtish, with a harsh and heckling voice, he was of an uncompromising ugliness which would have stopped most actors dead in their tracks from the outset. But the frog mouth, the speckled cheeks, the thin black patent-leather hair all made a vivid impression on Depression audiences. His very physical insignificance earned him attention in an age when the underdog was more of an underdog than he had ever been before. Moreover, Robinson played his villainous protagonist without a scintilla of compromise. By going back to Burnett's novel and stripping away the sentiment in the script * during daily arguments on the set, he showed the exact character of Capone to a public which

---

* Written by Francis Farago and Robert Lord, based on a first draft by Robert E. Lee.

had been fed only on garish headlines. When Bandello dies at the end, his final line, adapted from Burnett, "Mother of God (*mercy* in some versions), is this the end of Rico?" at once humanized the character and made his monstrousness seem convincingly pathetic. *Little Caesar* remained the matrix and the exemplar. And at one stroke it made Warner Brothers a great—rather than a merely opportunist—studio.

The success of the picture, following its opening at the Strand Theatre in New York, swept Warners into a wave of sociological dramas the like of which has not been seen in the history of Hollywood. First National, Vitagraph and Warners on Sunset worked at full capacity to produce the new genre. First, a companion piece to *Little Caesar, The Doorway to Hell,* was directed by the young Archie Mayo and written by Rowland Brown—a gifted director in his own right who had once served a term in jail—and George Rosener. It was notable for the introduction to important picture making of James Cagney, drawn, like Robinson, from the stage, and wasted by Warners hitherto; and for the serious miscasting of Lew Ayres, star of *All Quiet on the Western Front,* as the Bandello-like Italian gangster, Louis Ricarno.

The authenticity of the Warner crime pictures in the next two years stemmed in part from the writers. The most famous of these were Kubec Glasmon and John Bright, who wrote *Public Enemy, Blonde Crazy, Smart Money, Taxi* and several other major contributions to the cycle. Both men came from Chicago: Glasmon was a Polish emigré who ran a soda fountain of which Bright was the part-time soda jerk. Bright also worked as a young reporter on the *Chicago Evening Post,* dealing in stories of the criminal underground. Financed by Glasmon, Bright had even managed to write a biography of the iniquitous Mayor Thompson of Chicago. His hard-bitten style was also seen in a massive unpublished novel, rejected for censorship reasons by his publishers, Grosset and Dunlap, co-written with Glasmon and entitled *Beer and Blood*. Glasmon, to raise capital, deliberately paid two expert arsonists and explosion experts to destroy his soda fountain, and with the insurance money he and Bright went to Hollywood. There they lived in poverty until Rufus LeMaire, producer of "LeMaire's Affairs," a New York revue, who was in Los Angeles negotiating for a job of producer with Jack Warner, showed the manuscript to Zanuck. Zanuck virtually claimed the book as his own discovery, throwing LeMaire the bone of a job as casting director, which LeMaire held for several years. Jack Warner liked the material, and there was some talk of casting Eddie Woods in the important central role of a gangster, based on an actual figure in the Chicago underworld. But Glasmon and Bright wanted James Cagney and decided to push Zanuck to change his mind. The film was originally to have been directed by Archie Mayo, but Zanuck had just befriended an out of work director, William Wellman, a tough man's man with whom he liked to go hunting. When Wellman liked Cagney also, the matter was settled.

A brilliant actor with a thrusting, forceful style, Cagney was perfect for *Public Enemy*. The character of Tom, a cheap and ruthless hoodlum, was based by the co-authors upon people they knew in Chicago, and ever, supporting role, every situation in the plot, was authentic No attempt was made to glamorize Tom, the gangste Cagney played. At the end of the picture, he is delivered to his own home, lashed to a board in hospital clothing and falls forward through the front door. Entirely without compromise, the film was a definitive portrait of American crime, as close to the actual facts of Chicago mob activities as the writers dared.

The last sequence was destined to become famous: Cagney squashed a grapefruit in the face of his mistress, Mae Clarke. Miss Clarke was suffering from a severe cold, and came on the set asking Wellman if the shot could be faked. Wellman and Cagney assured her that the grapefruit would only approach her face; a special angle of the camera would give the impression that it had almost smothered her. She relaxed. Meanwhile, Cagney went into his dressing room and whittled off the edge of the grapefruit until it was sharp and jagged. A few moments later, the shot began. Without warning, Cagney not only thrust the grapefruit violently into Mae Clarke's face, he twisted it so that her nose bled. She screamed in genuine terror, tears streaming down her cheeks. The moment the shot was over, she rushed at Cagney and cried out, "Oh you son of a bitch, look what you did to me!" What he had done to her was to make her a star: the scene was magnificent, because her terror and misery were absolutely genuine.

Early in 1932, Warners bought *I Am a Fugitive from a Chain Gang*, the story of an escapee from a Georgia prison, Robert E. Burns, and ghostwritten by his brother, a clergyman, to engage sympathy for his cause. The original screenplay of *I Am a Fugitive* was written by the Broadway playwright Sheridan Gibney. Like John Bright and other Warner writers, Gibney was in his early twenties at the time, a man of great sophistication and intelligence whose Hollywood career ended in a blacklisting in the early 1950s. According to the terms of Burns' contract, he worked for four weeks with Gibney as an assistant on the script; terrified of recapture by the Georgia police, he stayed in Hollywood under an assumed name, and insisted upon armed protection around the clock. After Gibney had interviewed Burns, and listened to his protestations of innocence, he began to feel certain that the man was guilty; and Gibney sensed a powerful feeling of violence underlying the calm exterior of the small and weak creature who sat working with him day after day. When a crime film was shot in an adjoining lot, Burns cowered in terror at the sound of police sirens, picked up his hat and ran into the street. It was an uncomfortable association, and Gibney was relieved when it ended.

Gibney left for New York, where he prepared a Broadway play. When Zanuck called him for rewrites, he was not available, and Zanuck immediately dismissed him from the studio payroll, hiring two other writers to recast a few pages of his material. Mervyn LeRoy was chosen to direct, and Paul Muni to star in the part of Burns. Made with uncompromising realism, the film was a fine addition to the crime series, a cool recreation of the horror of the Georgia prisons. The fade-out as written in Gibney's original script and directed by LeRoy was unforgettable. Reduced to an unshaven, hungry wreck, Muni is hiding in an alleyway when a girl asks, "How do you live?" and he replies, "I steal." The scene was shot in downtown Los Angeles. LeRoy rehearsed the scene with half the lights in the alley lit up. Just as Muni spoke the line, there was a convenient power failure. In the final shot the fugitive runs off into complete darkness, and is swallowed up.

After the film was released, there was so widespread a public outcry that chains were removed from prisoners throughout Georgia. At the same time, various Georgian officials warned Warners not to risk entering the state at any time; the state sued the brothers for defamation, and two Georgia prison wardens lodged their own suit for libel. All of these suits were settled out of court.

I Am a Fugitive from a Chain Gang not only confirmed LeRoy's talent, it established still further the Warner Brothers' claim to be providing genuine social commentary, aggressive, liberal, genuinely reformist. Their revelations of criminal methods aided clean-up campaigns in Chicago and New York, their slicing through the realities of newspaper life were valuable in improving the quality of the papers they symbolically denounced, and the removal of chains from Georgia prisoners, and from other convicts in the Deep South, alone made them the most important studio after M-G-M in Hollywood.

Mervyn LeRoy's *Five Star Final* followed quickly, by Byron Morgan and Robert Lord, based on Louis Weitzenkorn's autobiographical Broadway play exposing the wickedness of a scandal sheet in gathering news, in exploiting the unfortunate. The boss of a yellow newspaper which employs Robinson as its editor decides to revive an account of an old murder case as part of a circulation stunt. The woman accused of murder is now the mother of a virginal young girl, and is so distressed at the possibility of her daughter discovering the truth, she commits suicide. Finally, Robinson turns on his employers and, for the benefit of the masses, analyzes precisely what is evil about American journalism. Although the scenes involving the unhappy mother (played by the Belasco luminary Frances Starr) and her husband (H. B. Warner) were excessively maudlin, the newspaper sequences had considerable power. The playing of Robinson as Randall, the overworked, dishonest editor still capable of seeing the truth, was magnificent, brilliantly right for the new camera techniques of the period, laying down the whole foundation of movie acting technique in the talkies for forty years to come.

Another important film of the period, generally overlooked, was *The Mouthpiece* (1932), co-directed by Lubitsch's former assistant, James Flood, and Elliott Nugent. Earl Baldwin's adaptation of Frank J. Collins' play opens with the prosecutor Vincent Day, played by Warren William, closing a strongly argued address to the jury which results in the execution of an innocent boy. Abandoning all decency, Day becomes a "front man" for a gangster mob; the portrait of gang life and, of crooked lawyers, of bribes to the judge, is pitilessly drawn and Warren Wil-

95

liam plays with an agreeable stylized, almost Bar-
rymorean flair.

In 1933, Michael Curtiz made *20,000 Years in Sing
Sing*, a film which, in common with its predecessors, was
drawn from an account of actual events: in this case, a
book by Warden Louis E. Lawes about life in that particular prison, adapted by Wilson Mizner * and Brown
Holmes and readapted by Courtnay Terrett and Robert
Lord. It was the story of a hardened criminal, played by
Spencer Tracy, who is gradually led into sensitivity and
understanding by the warden, played by Arthur Byron;
Tracy's girlfriend was played with striking intensity by
the young Bette Davis. As in so many Warner films of the
time, not only does the film offer a forceful, uncluttered
exposition but a powerful closing line, rivalling "I steal"
in *I Am a Fugitive from a Chain Gang.* Following the announcement on the radio of Tracy's death in the electric
chair, Ted Lewis provides his familiar radio line, "Is everybody happy?" The irony, obvious but affecting, was
pure "Warner Brothers."

Alongside the films which dealt explicitly with crime
and were drawn from actual reports, there were numerous
films which depicted sympathetically the life of the poor
and the downtrodden without specifically dealing in criminal types. An admirable example of this genre was Mervyn LeRoy's film *Two Seconds* (1932), adapted by Harvey
Thew from the play by Elliott Lester. It was the story of a
poor and unhappy man, a prototype played with his customary intensity by Edward G. Robinson, who is pushed
into a position where he is forced to kill his wife, and dies
in the electric chair. During the two seconds between his
seating in the chair and his electrocution, the little man
relives his life of suffering, defeat, and despair. The film

---

* Mizner, though incapable of writing dialogue of quality, was a
gifted "constructionist"—i.e., film plotter, of that time.

provided a vivid illumination of the mid-Depression: like a fly-specked bulb, it lit up a life of sordid hopelessness. The central figure is so short and so ugly that he has lost his sexual pride. Arriving at a 10-cents-a-dance hall, he seedily runs his eye over the pathetic and down-at-heel prostitutes, lined up for his inspection. One of these, played with brilliant precision by Vivienne Osborne, shanghais him into a shotgun marriage, with a teacup handle used as a wedding ring. Harvey Thew's script, carefully expanding the play, contains sharply observant lines, all of which serve to give us a picture without compromise.

Mervyn LeRoy's unpretentious, inartistic but forceful directing also attracted attention in *Three on a Match*, made, with five other pictures, in 1932.* Lucien Hubbard, known chiefly as a director, wrote the screenplay from a story by the prolific Kubec Glasmon and John Bright. It was the tale of three girls from the slums who meet years later: one, played by Bette Davis, is a secretary; another, played by Joan Blondell, is a showgirl; and a third, played by the admirable Ann Dvorak, is a rich socialite. Once more, the exposition is as swift as in a good tabloid newspaper story, the dialogue full of wisecracks and the inevitable "Gee you're swells" hitting off as always the precise quality of America, with all of the raucous humor, the enthusiasm, the toughness, the frank sexuality which characterized proletarian society in the era.

Warners did not neglect the problems of women. In 1930–1933, the Warners presented the new and remarkably gifted Broadway actress Barbara Stanwyck in a series of raw melodramas specifically designed for women: forerunners, in fact, of the Warners women's pictures of a decade later. In Archie Mayo's *Illicit,* Miss Stanwyck played

---

* The others were *Heart of New York, Elmer the Great, The World Changes, High Pressure* and *Big City Blues.*

a girl who risked being socially ostracized by living openly with her lover. In *Night Nurse*, she was shown as a struggling girl who discovers, in a vividly realized hospital milieu, the horror and gallows wit of medical life. A companion piece was Lloyd Bacon's *Miss Pinkerton*, about another nurse as hard-bitten as the one she played in Wellman's film turning detective and flushing out the secret of a murder case. The whole lowlife realism cycle was obviously a tremendously successful one, and the films, during 1932 and 1933, poured off the assembly line with astonishing frequency.

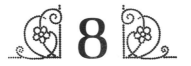

8

Return to
the Musical

Whaile the lowlife cycle flourished—together with a related series of horror-crime films, including Michael Curtiz' *The Mystery of the Wax Museum* and *Dr. X*—the company continued to have a series of upheavals at the outset of the 1930s. Harry Warner brilliantly manipulated Warners' own stock, through Schatzkin and Company, his principal brokers, profiting personally from this arrangement by $9,251,454.50 in one year. Harry simply bought the stock when it was depressed and sold it when company profits began to rise, a perfectly legal maneuver at the time. The intention was simply to provide large sums which could be loaned to the company from Harry's own funds: during 1930, Warner supplied Warners-First National with almost 12 million dollars, repaid in debentures of the company.

But despite these, and similar ingenious efforts, the company still headed on into stormy waters in 1931, its enormous investment in the Stanley theatre chain proving an intolerable burden. The expansion continued: on January 7, 1931, the executive staff was consolidated under one roof at Burbank, with the Sunset Boulevard studio, Warner Ranch and the old Vitagraph studio used as auxiliary plants. In the reshuffle, Spyros and George Skouras, who had temporarily joined the company after the purchase of their theatres, resigned. Darryl Zanuck became executive in charge of production, with Hal Wallis and Lucien Hubbard as associate executives, William Koenig continuing as general studio manager and Robert Lord, Raymond Griffith and Henry Blanke as production executives.

That year, the company lost $500,066.44 in the first quarter alone, thus proving that the public was again beginning to cut down on its film-going habits. The Brunswick Radio Corporation and National Radio Advertising Incorporated—both subsidiaries of the company—lost $1,269,275.63. On December 1, 1931, Warners cut salaries from 20 to 30 percent; all of their employees were told that unless they accepted the situation they would be out of work. Since most of the players would have faced hardship, or at best a $75 a week job on Broadway, and since many had families to support, there were no resignations. Bette Davis, Joan Blondell, Edward G. Robinson and the very rebellious James Cagney had to swallow their anger, at least for the time being, and struggle along as best they could with schedules and salaries incommensurate with their international fame. On July 25, 1932, Jack Warner and Darryl Zanuck issued a joint statement to the effect that in the future no star would be permitted to have any say at all in any aspect of a production, including the selection of a story. A few days later, further salary cuts were made. In August, 1932, despite these stringencies, the company announced a loss of $8,242,755. Cagney walked out of the studio in April, disgusted by his poor income of $1400 a week (it was still much greater than that of stars such as the unfortunate Joan Blondell, who was receiving only $250 a week). After arbitration by the Academy of Arts and Sciences in September, Cagney was restored to his position with an increase to $1750 a week.

At the end of 1932, shareholders were again disaffected, repeating their earlier charge that the Warners were draining money from their company to feather their personal nests. A resurgent group including Max Goldberg of Goldberg and Goldberg of Salem, Massachusetts, headed a proxy fight in Wilmington, Delaware; at a stormy meeting, Goldberg announced that he had proxies of 4000 stockholders owning some 400,000 shares, and demanded that there be a full investigation of the company's affairs and a new board of directors. But Harry Warner, leading the brothers into battle, firmly quashed the attempt.

By 1933, the company's financial situation had worsened. There even seemed to be the further possibility of a strike by disaffected players; tension reached a peak on March 6, when all the employees of Warners and of the other film studios took a 50 percent salary cut for a period of eight weeks. The emergency board of the Academy of Motion Picture Arts and Sciences announced that Warners must restore full salaries, and the brothers refused. The board adopted a resolution charging breach of the agreement and advising the staff they could obtain retroactive payment to March 6. Again the brothers refused to comply. Darryl Zanuck, exasperated by the situation and also enjoying a handsome offer from Joe Schenck, resigned his position as head of production on April 15, 1933, and the players began to talk about taking Warners to court if they did not accede to the Academy's ruling.

Ten days after Zanuck left, losing $5000 a week salary, Warners gave in anyway.

Before he left Warners for an extraordinary career at the studio which became Twentieth Century-Fox, Zanuck had instituted a policy of reviving the musical genre which had been virtually killed off in 1930. The musicals further increased the reputation of the brothers as makers of important entertainment pictures, although ironically Zanuck obtained little or no credit for reviving the genre.

The principles behind the new wave of musicals were exactly the same as those which ruled the wave of crime, lowlife and horror films: tight budgets, a driving pace, scenes shot wherever possible in one take and with one camera, sets lit so that they looked twice as substantial as they were, writers compelled to have every line and every situation perfect on each day of shooting. The cast still rose at five every morning, started work at eight after makeup and run-throughs, and often continued until midnight. On Saturdays, as before, they worked all through the night. Despite a diet consisting largely of hamburgers, cokes, and hard liquor, somehow they managed to sustain the energy to toil arduously through the complicated dance routines, the involved comedy situations, the rat-tat-tat confrontations of the dramatic episodes.

Under Hal Wallis, the skillful Busby Berkeley spent 18 hours a day perfecting the presentations of the dance sequences. An irascible genius, with the voice and manner of a roughneck, Berkeley personally selected the girls, and dreamed up the dances on the set. Unable to choreograph or to dance himself, he simply visualized the arrangements of the girls, frequently in snowflake formations or as the petals of grotesque flowers, and his assistants carried his ideas out on the floor. He also worked very closely with the art director Anton Grot, who designed sets which were in a sense reflections of Berkeley's erotic dreams.

In 1933, Warners decided to remake *The Gold Diggers* yet again, under the co-direction of Berkeley and Mervyn LeRoy. Sound Stage Seven was lifted 40 feet in order to achieve the remarkable sweeping shots which were a distinctive feature of the production. On Berkeley's advice cameras were placed on the catwalks alongside the arc lights, to achieve many ingenious shots using special wide-angle lenses. In endless conferences and rehearsals, the complex details were worked out. During the production, the Long Beach earthquake took place: the girls playing neon lit violins (an idea of Mervyn LeRoy's) with wires under their clothes in the Shadow Waltz scene short circuited, and a number of girls almost fell off their perches above the stage. LeRoy was on a parallel near the camera and almost fell to his death. Berkeley yelled out to the girls to sit down and not to jump; if they did, they would kill themselves. The whole sound stage was plunged in darkness. Amid the screams and cries and falls, Jack Warner arrived, and made it clear to Berkeley that the shooting would have to continue; and it did, until one o'clock the following morning.

Another great musical of the period was *42nd Street*, magnificently directed by Lloyd Bacon, written by Rian James and James Seymour from the novel by Bradford Ropes, incorporating elements from *On with the Show*, with music and lyrics by Harry Warren and Al Dubin. The story of a falling star, played by Bebe Daniels, whose broken leg gives an opportunity to Ruby Keeler to make good, and of a driving stage producer, Julian Marsh, dying of heart disease (Warren Baxter), based on Ziegfeld's great director Julian Mitchell, may have been a product of the dramatic cornbelt, but the dialogue, racy and unsentimental, and the bringing together of the physical elements were beyond praise. The cast was deeply affecting: Ginger Rogers' tough, gum-chewing and monocled showgirl, Bebe Daniels' grandiose idol of the theatre,

Warren Baxter's sick and unhappy Julian Marsh totally committed to the stage.

42nd Street is important because, in common with the crime thrillers, it gives an extraordinarily accurate portrait of one segment of American life. Unlike most musicals, it presents a remarkably frank, savage and earthy picture of the world backstage. No nonsense here about "glamor": chorus girls are little more than prostitutes, using their bodies for better opportunities in the show, raucously assessing the main chance; dance directors select their sexual favorites from lines of hopefuls; money and desire are the only motivations of a life devoid of beauty, wit or culture. When a musical number in the show illustrates Forty-Second Street, we see a chiaroscuro of violence, squalor and lust; when an angry landlady orders a man out of a girl's lodging house room, another girl in a slip sends her lover packing behind the landlady's back. The sweat, grit and misery of creating a show is not glossed over; a young girl struggling for a break collapses from exhaustion; the sick producer, in a final shot devoid of all romance, sinks worn out on the steps of a fire escape next to the theatre in Atlantic City, as members of the preview audience walk past him commenting on the show. Another studio would have provided a final close-up of the lovers played by George Brent and Bebe Daniels at the altar during their wedding, while Ruby Keeler and Dick Powell, who have just discovered each other, wander along 42nd Street hand in hand crooning cheerfully for the fade-out. Not this studio: the ending is a portrait of futility, a shot of a doomed man, accompanied by the chattering of a theatre crowd.

The cycle continued briskly with *Dames,* made in 1934, directed by Ray Enright. The film dealt with the activities of a bizarre millionaire, Ezra Ounce, played by Hugh Herbert, in his efforts to raise the moral standards of the United States: he despises the theatre and the cinema, believes sex to be evil even when sanctified by the vows of marriage, and has a horror of show people. The humor today seems painfully strained, but the screenplay, based by Delmer Daves on a story by Robert Lord and Daves himself, is constructed with great skill, and the musical numbers of Busby Berkeley have their customary vulgar magnificence. Ray Enright also directed in that year *20 Million Sweethearts*, with Dick Powell, Pat O'Brien and Ginger Rogers; an intelligent satire on radio, written by Warren Duff and Harry Sauber from material by Jerry Wald and J. F. Moss, it was the story of a singing waiter, played by Powell, whom Pat O'Brien discovers for success on the air. The film—like *Dames* before it—further established the popularity of Dick Powell, whose bright manner, sophomoric polished-cheekbone looks, and cropped hair were precisely right for the dream requirements of females at that time.

It would be tedious to enumerate all of the many musicals which Warners made at the time, though of the others *Footlight Parade,* again chiefly due to Busby Berkeley's contribution, was certainly important. Unfortunately, just as the gangster genre became severely stereotyped by 1935 (William Keighley's *G-Men* was a case in point) so the musical, with its crude comedy, its snappy secretaries, idiotic sugar daddies, scheming gold diggers and hard-bitten theatrical producers began to look distinctly shopworn only two years after the revival of the mode. The real trouble was that Warners, in its excitement over the success of crime film, lowlife film and musical in turn, simply wrang out the formulaes as soon as they were developed. It was typical of Hollywood as a whole, overexploiting successful subjects, failing to come up with sufficient variety in its factory products.

In 1935, Hal Wallis, who had developed from being a genial, outgoing publicity man into a shrewd, tightfisted producer with much of the drive of Zanuck, decided on a change of pace. He began with Jack Warner's approval to institute a policy of "prestige pictures," epics, and historical biographies. From the beginning, of course, Warners had flirted with "culture": in its adaptations during the silent period of Sinclair Lewis and Edith Wharton, in an early sound biography of Disraeli with George Arliss, in a version of Gerald Du Maurier's *Trilby* (*Svengali*, with John Barrymore, 1931), in a curiosity directed by William Dieterle, *Scarlet Dawn*, a travesty of the Russian Revolution in which Kay Francis played Lenin's secretary. Dieterle's film *The Last Flight*, from a script by John Monk Saunders, who had also written *Wings*, was a Scott Fitzgerald-like work of great intensity, set in Paris following the ruined careers of airmen who had dropped out of sight after performing feats of heroism in World War I. Since Dieterle, once a distinguished actor on the Berlin stage and in UFA films, now an authoritative and forceful man of commanding height and daunting presence, seemed to represent the studio's rare bids for intellectual respectability, it was only natural that he should be the prime figure in its "cultural" period. Alongside him stood the writer Sheridan Gibney, another German emigré, Lubitsch's former assistant, the witty and charming Henry Blanke, the Polish Anton Grot, and even, at the outset, that extraordinary man of the theatre, his former employer Max Reinhardt.

Marie Prévost and Adolphe Menjou being directed by Lubitsch, for "The Marriage Circle." © Warner Brothers 1923 Copyright Renewed.

Rin-Tin-Tin, in "The Lighthouse by the Sea." © Warner Bros. 1924 Copyright Renewed.

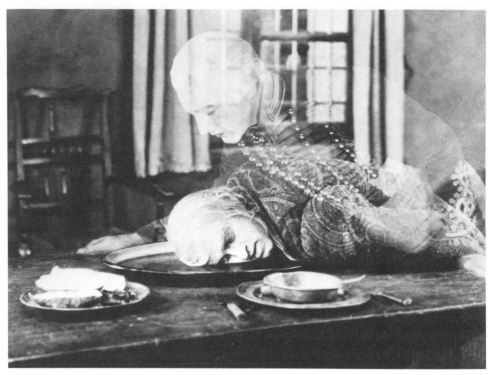

John Barrymore in "Beau Brummell." © Warner Bros. Pictures Inc. 1924 Copyright Renewed.

Beverly Bayne and Edith Roberts in "The Age of Innocence." © Warner Bros. Pictures, Inc. 1924 Copyright Renewed.

John Barrymore in "The Sea Beast." © Warner Bros. Pictures, Inc.
1925 Copyright Renewed.

John Barrymore and Montagu Love in "Don Juan." © Warner Bros.
Pictures, Inc. 1926 Copyright Renewed.

A Tribute to the Warner Brothers

JACK L. WARNER

ALBERT WARNER

SAM L. WARNER

After tonight's premiere the hats of the discriminating first nighters will be off to Warner brothers, for having given to the screen such a gem of dramatic artistry as "Don Juan."

These producers of vision and foresight spared no expense to make this triumph of

John Barrymore's a production that will stand the test of time and bring the utmost in cinema enjoyment to all who are fortunate enough to see it.

I know this evening's audience will join me in heartiest congratulations.

SID GRAUMAN

HARRY M. WARNER

From the Don Juan program.

Dolores Costello, Warner Oland, Anna May Wong in "Old San Francisco." © Warner Bros. Pictures, Inc. 1927 Copyright Renewed.

Al Jolson in "The Jazz Singer." © Warner Bros. Pictures, Inc. 1927 Copyright Renewed.

Carlotta King and John Boles in "The Desert Song." © Warner Bros. Pictures, Inc. 1929 Copyright Renewed.

Flood scene from "Noah's Ark." © Warner Bros. Pictures, Inc. 1929 Copyright Renewed.

Ethel Waters in "On With the Show." © Warner Bros. Pictures, Inc. 1929 Copyright Renewed.

"Lady Luck" Production Number from "The Show of Shows." © Warner Bros. Pictures, Inc. 1929 Copyright Renewed.

Edward G. Robinson, George E. Stone and Stanley Fields in "Little Caesar." © First National Pictures, Inc. 1930 Copyright Renewed.

Donald Cook, James Cagney in "Public Enemy." © Warner Bros. Pictures, Inc. 1931 Copyright Renewed.

Mary Astor and Humphrey Bogart in "The Maltese Falcon." © Warner Bros. Pictures, Inc. 1941 Copyright Renewed.

George E. Stone, Edward G. Robinson in "Five Star Final." © First National Pictures, Inc. 1931 Copyright Renewed.

Bette Davis, Joan Blondell and Ann Dvorak in "Three On a Match." ©
First National Pictures, Inc. 1932 Copyright Renewed.

Paul Muni in "I Am a Fugitive from a Chain Gang." © Warner Bros.
Pictures, Inc. 1932 Copyright Renewed.

George E. Stone, Dick Powell, Bebe Daniels, Warner Baxter, Una Merkel in "42nd Street." © Warner Bros. Pictures, Inc. 1933 Copyright Renewed.

Olivia de Havilland and Errol Flynn in "Captain Blood." © Warner Bros. Pictures, Inc. 1935 Copyright Renewed.

*Humphrey Bogart in "Black Legion." © Warner Bros. Pictures, Inc. &
The Vitaphone Corp. 1936 Copyright Renewed.*

*Claude Rains in "They Won't Forget." © Warner Bros. Pictures, Inc.
1937 Copyright Renewed.*

Bette Davis and Henry Fonda in "Jezebel." © Warner Bros. Pictures, Inc. 1938 Copyright Renewed.

Basil Rathbone, Claude Rains, Olivia de Havilland, Errol Flynn in "The Adventures of Robin Hood." © Warner Bros. Pictures, Inc. 1938 Copyright Renewed.

Errol Flynn in "The Adventures of Robin Hood." © Warner Bros. Pictures, Inc. 1938 Copyright Renewed.

Ronald Reagan, Bette Davis in "Dark Victory." © Warner Bros. Pictures, Inc. 1939 Copyright Renewed.

Bette Davis and Geraldine Fitzgerald in "Dark Victory." © Warner Bros. Pictures, Inc. 1939 Copyright Renewed.

Henry O'Neill, Edward G. Robinson in "Confessions of a Nazi Spy." ©
Warner Bros. Pictures, Inc. 1939 Copyright Renewed.

31.

Bette Davis and Errol
Flynn in "The Private
Lives of Elizabeth and
Essex." © Warner
Bros. Pictures, Inc.
1939 Copyright
Renewed.

Mary Astor and Bette Davis in "The Great Lie." © Warner Bros. Pictures, Inc. 1941 Copyright Renewed.

Errol Flynn, Flora Robson, Brenda Marshall in "The Sea Hawk." © Warner Bros. Pictures, Inc. 1940 Copyright Renewed.

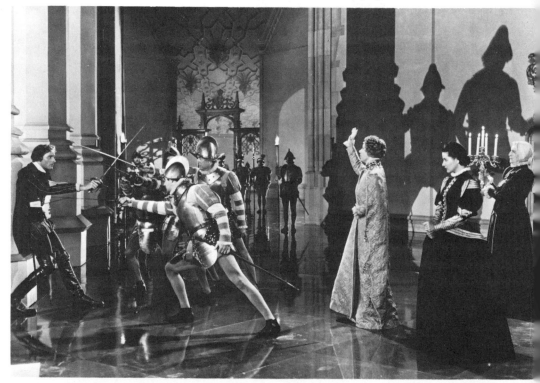

Gary Cooper in "Sergeant York." © *Warner Bros. Pictures, Inc. 1941*
Copyright Renewed.

Paul Henreid and Bette Davis in "Now, Voyager." © *Warner Bros. Pictures, Inc. 1942 Copyright Renewed.*

Humphrey Bogart and Ingrid Bergman in "Casablanca." © Warner Bros. Pictures, Inc. 1943 Copyright Renewed.

Helmut Dantine, Moroni Olsen, Ann Harding, Minor Watson, Eleanor Parker, Walter Huston in "Mission to Moscow." © Warner Bros. Pictures, Inc. 1943 Copyright Renewed.

Errol Flynn, Julie Bishop, Gene Lockhart, Helmut Dantine in "Northern Pursuit." © Warner Bros. Pictures, Inc. 1943 Copyright Renewed.

Humphrey Bogart and Sydney Greenstreet in "Passage to Marseille." © Warner Bros. Pictures, Inc. 1944 Copyright Renewed.

*Lauren Bacall and Humphrey Bogart in "To Have and Have Not." ©
Warner Bros. Pictures, Inc. Copyright Renewed.*

*Jack Carson, Joan Crawford and Ann Blyth in "Mildred Pierce." ©
Warner Bros. Pictures, Inc. 1945 Copyright Renewed.*

Bette Davis and Bette Davis in "A Stolen Life." © Warner Bros. Pictures, Inc. 1946 Copyright Renewed.

Dorothy Malone and Humphrey Bogart in "The Big Sleep." © Warner Bros. Pictures, Inc. 1946 Copyright Renewed.

Bette Davis and Claude Rains in "Deception." © Warner Bros. Pictures, Inc. 1946 Copyright Renewed.

Ann Sheridan in "Nora Prentiss." © Warner Bros. Pictures, Inc. 1947 Copyright Renewed.

James Stewart, Farley Granger, Constance Collier, Joan Chandler, Sir Cedric Hardwicke, John Dall, Douglas Dick in "Rope." © Transatlantic Pictures Corp. 1948.

Patricia Neal, Gary Cooper in "The Fountainhead." © Warner Bros. Pictures, Inc. 1949 Copyright Renewed.

James Cagney in "White Heat." © Warner Bros. Pictures, Inc. 1949 Copyright Renewed.

Hope Emerson, Eleanor Parker, Betty Garde in the motion picture "Caged" courtesy of Warner Bros.-Seven Arts, Inc. copyright © 1950

Kirk Douglas and Hoagy Carmichael in the motion picture "Young Man with a Horn" courtesy of Warner Bros.-Seven Arts, Inc. copyright © 1950

Steve Cochran, Joan Crawford and Selena Royle in the motion picture "Damned Don't Cry" courtesy of Warner Bros.-Seven Arts, Inc. copyright © 1950

Robert Middleton, Steve Cochran, Doris Day, Ginger Rogers in the
motion picture "Storm Warning" courtesy of Warner Bros.-Seven Arts,
Inc. copyright © 1951

Judy Garland and James Mason in the motion picture "A Star Is Born"
courtesy of Warner Bros.-Seven Arts, Inc. copyright © 1954

James Mason, Judy Garland, Charles Bickford in the motion picture "A Star Is Born" courtesy of Warner Bros.-Seven Arts, Inc. copyright © 1954

James Dean in the motion picture "Rebel Without a Cause" courtesy of Warner Bros.-Seven Arts, Inc. copyright © 1955

Richard Davalos, James Dean and Jo Van Fleet in the motion picture "East of Eden" courtesy of Warner Bros.-Seven Arts, Inc. copyright © 1955

James Dean in the motion picture "Giant" courtesy of Warner Bros.-Seven Arts, Inc. copyright © 1956

Prestige
Pictures

ANYONE WANDERING IN-
to Warner Brothers in the mid-1930s would have been for-
given for thinking himself in a madhouse. All the sound
stages, recording and cutting rooms were hives of activity. Writers were pounding their typewriters angrily in
their tiny cubbyholes. Everywhere, quarrels broke out,
marked by foul language and threats of violence. At the
head of the operation, Jack Warner continued to be as hu-
morous, hard-bitten and determined as ever, with the as-
tute Hal Wallis as his expert second-in-command. The
chief directors were all extraordinarily irascible, difficult,
overbearing men: Michael Curtiz, with his malapropish
Hungarian use of language and whipcrack voice; Anatole
Litvak, equally ill-tempered, squabbling endlessly with
his writers and stars; William Dieterle, proud and stub-

born, directing with a leaden hand. Only the writers, intelligent men like Seton I. Miller and Milton Krims, the actors and some of the producers, among them Robert Lord and Henry Blanke, managed to keep a level head.

Yet despite the appearance of chaos, Warners was by 1936 a very well-oiled machine, with each department functioning effectively in an interlocking structure. The technical departments were at their peak: the art directors Anton Grot, Carl Jules Weyl and Robert Haas, with their teams of draftsmen, the cameramen, led by Hal Mohr, Sol Polito, Tony Gaudio, Ernest Haller; the editors, including such gifted men as George Amy and Ralph Dawson; the sound recorders, still under Major Nathan Levinson and George Groves; the music department under Leo F. Forbstein: few studios could match the efficiency and doggedness of these masters of their craft.

The system of picture-making at Warners was by now firmly laid down. Gone were the days in which a man like Lubitsch could make his own rules; never again would a genius of this caliber be able to work at the studio. A Welles or an Eisenstein would have been crushed at once by the system. The writers, encouraged by Hal Wallis, unquestionably occupied first place: they set the entire tone of the pictures of the time. The scripts were prepared in detail, even down to specific compositions of the shots, and the writers were almost invariably present on the sets during the shooting. Once a producer had approved a finished screenplay, he cast the stars of the picture. The director was called in, and in rare instances helped with casting of minor roles or changes in the writing. For economic reasons, he had orders to rehearse his players, then only use one take for a scene. The producer or studio manager selected the art directors, the composers, the cameramen, the cutters. These were seldom the choice of the directors, and all conformed to studio style: the bold low-key lighting, the rich emphatic music, the quick cutting, the economical sets which were blanketed in shadows to look far more expensive than they were.

Despite the quarrels, the actors, writers and technicians formed a genial and prideful team. Working for a factory, they imparted to their work a remarkable drive. They gave Warner pictures a magic, a murky sophisticated poetry, that made their films highly individual in a standardized industry.

Sometime in the mid-1930s, the American public became obsessed with "culture," began buying European novels and solid biographies, and began looking for picaresque romances in which the characters constantly talked about philosophy, religion and the hereafter. The size of the book had to be that of the average brick, the prose as chunky and unmanageable as possible, giving an illusion of "literature." The story department decided not so much to buy up the available books as to provide "moving picture books" drawn from Shakespeare or from the lives of actual people of distinction. So, automatically, a "culture cycle" began: in 1934, Max Reinhardt, then producing the play at the Hollywood Bowl for the Los Angeles Chamber of Commerce, was engaged by Henry Blanke to do *A Midsummer Night's Dream*. Blanke obtained Jack Warner's permission to go ahead with William Dieterle as co-director. The entire venture turned out to be a disaster.

In the first place, the film suffered from a graceless and clumsy cast, led by Victor Jory as Oberon and Anita Louise as a simpering Titania; the clowns, led by James Cagney, were disagreeably coarse; and Mickey Rooney, as Puck, broke his leg during the shooting, forcing him to be pushed rather obviously up and down behind bushes on a tricycle. Worse, Reinhardt and his associate director William Dieterle quarrelled incessantly. Reinhardt's sense of magic and wonder was constantly weighed down by Deiterle's elephantinely ponderous and clumsy direction of the cast.

But the most serious blow came after three weeks of shooting: most of the film could not be seen at the rushes at all, and Jack Warner became horrified by the darkness of the images. The problem lay in the art direction. With Reinhardt's and Dieterle's approval, Anton Grot had designed a forest which extended over two adjoining sound stages—a fantastic fairy-tale creation as fine as anything in the illustrations of Doré, Dulac or Griffenhagen. The trees were made of burlap dipped in a plaster of Paris solution, and the leaves were real, stuck on by hand one by one, and sprayed with silver paint. The moss also was real, and had to be watered with the utmost care each day.

The great forest had only one disadvantage: it could not be photographed. Within the then existing framelines, only portions of the trees with their massive trunks and twisting Gothic branches could be seen, and after several weeks of painfully difficult work by the cameraman Ernest Haller, some of whose effects were so dark they could barely be developed in the laboratories, Jack Warner came close to cancelling production.

In an attempt to save the picture, Dieterle selected a new cameraman, Hal Mohr, a master of the use of light who had already distinguished himself in some of the famous Warner films of the changeover period. Mohr had only to glance at the set to see that the forest simply could not be filmed as it stood. He asked for a weekend to have the entire set changed, and Hal Wallis gave him permission to retain a team of painters, greenmen, and carpenters. They worked, with brief breaks for meals, all through Saturday, Saturday night and Sunday until Monday morning. Under Mohr's meticulous supervision, the tops of all the trees were cut off, some branches were removed because they obstructed all of the arc lights, and Haller's complete lighting system was revised. (Haller had attempted to show light coming from a number of sources, but Mohr, more naturalistically, had light coming from the same source, streaming in sunbeams or moonbeams from a bank of lights which were placed at one end of the stage.)

Mohr arranged for a team with spray guns filled with aluminum paint to cover the trees from one side. He used orange shellac on the other. The result was a strikingly realistic visual effect, showing bright sunlight and deep shadows—orange being an impenetrable color, photographing black. Special-effects men with cobweb machines covered all of the trees, bushes and grass under Mohr's supervision. He also used "casket fillers," small metal particles which could reflect the available light. When Anton Grot came in on Monday morning, he was horrified at the results, but they photographed far better than before.

Aside from the photography this somewhat labored and Germanic production was a failure. The use of the Mendelssohn music also alienated the Depression public. Undaunted, Wallis and Henry Blanke insisted that the "cultural" cycle should proceed with biographies of famous men. For months, Blanke worked with Edward Chodorov on a screenplay of the life of Louis Pasteur, but the script was a disaster.

The idea was dropped, and picked up again, by a contract writer, Pierre Collings, who had been fascinated by the subject of medical research following a long battle against drug addiction which killed him only two years later. In 1935 he prepared a synopsis of the outstanding events in Pasteur's career, culminating in the development of specific drugs. Hal Wallis called in Sheridan Gibney, who had managed to return to the studio following his earlier dismissal, and asked him if he felt the material could be worked upon. Gibney scanned it carefully and felt that it would be ideal for Paul Muni, who shared his enthusiasm. During a discussion at Muni's walnut ranch in the San Fernando Valley, Gibney and Muni developed a number of ideas. Enthusiastic, Muni told Wallis he very much wanted to play the role of Pasteur; since the new Muni contract offered full-story approval, Wallis decided to engage Gibney to prepare the first draft of a screenplay.

By now, Collings was too seriously ill to work on the material, and Gibney proceeded alone. With the permission of Wallis and Blanke, Gibney was allowed to go to the Los Angeles County Hospital and arrange for slides to be made of anthrax cultures and to study various experiments which had their origin in Pasteur's research techniques. He read dozens of books and received files of material, filling him in on important details.

Muni deeply admired the finished script, which Blanke sent by messenger to Wallis in Canada where he was enjoying a brief vacation. According to Gibney, Wallis hated the material and telegraphed Jack Warner to have Gibney removed from the film at once, and replaced by another writer, Laird Doyle.

Muni exercised the power of his contract to have final choice on all subjects, and when he heard of Wallis' wire, he took a pen and wrote in his bold hand across the front cover of the script: *OK. MUNI.* Both Wallis and Jack Warner were furious. Warner called Muni to his office and carpeted him for an hour and a half, shouting that he was guilty of insubordination. As a form of punishment Warner and Wallis accorded the film the lowest possible budget figure ($330,000), used only contract players, and insisted upon the conversion of old musical film sets for the Louvre and the French court. The laboratory used by Lionel Atwill as the mad scientist in *The Mystery of the Wax Museum* became Louis Pasteur's with some minor changes and a fresh coat of paint. William Dieterle, who disliked the script intensely, was forced by the Warners to direct the picture as quickly and carelessly as possible. It was a desperately unhappy experience for all concerned.

Later, Warner shared Wallis' objections to the script: that it had no love story and dealt with the career of a man in whom nobody at the time could possibly be interested. He also agreed with Wallis that the film would antagonize the medical profession and would ruin Muni's career as he would be disguised throughout in a beard. "He looks like a Rabbi," he said. Gibney was dismissed at once.

In spite of everything, the ponderous and self-consciously worthy film was somewhat of a critical and commercial success, and won both Sheridan Gibney, who was now out of work, and the seriously ill Pierre Collings ironical Oscars. By an irony also not appealing to Gibney, the film earned Jack Warner a lasting reputation in France, and the award of the Légion d'Honneur, for having created a work for which, according to Gibney, he was in no sense responsible.

The moment *The Story of Louis Pasteur* succeeded, Jack Warner and Hal Wallis abandoned their original complaints against starring Muni in films of this kind, decently admitted their mistake, and cast him at once in another picture in which he played an impassioned advocate of the causes of honesty and decency. When the German and Hungarian playwrights Heinz Herald and Geza Herczeg took the story of Emile Zola and his struggle for the restitution of Captain Alfred Dreyfus to Lubitsch at M-G-M, Lubitsch suggested they pass it over to Henry Blanke. Blanke and Hal Wallis together ordered the most splendid production made by Warners up to that time, *The Life of Emile Zola*. Dieterle was again hired to direct. Anton Grot surpassed himself, completely blotting out the disgrace of A *Midsummer Night's Dream*, in recreating the Parisian houses of Dreyfus and Zola, the French court, the army barracks, the lonely prison on Devil's Island where Dreyfus was exiled. Norman Reilly

Raine, a first-rate writer, was engaged to prepare the script with Herald and Herczeg.

Muni was magnificent. As Zola, his personal qualities of intensity, thrusting honesty, and compulsive edgy drive were ideally employed in his portrait of the shambling, uncomfortable figure who devoted his career to the pursuit of truth. The actor's touches—the dangling spectacles, the constant searching for handkerchiefs in the wrong pockets, the struggling through the veil of a cold to a moment of wisdom—remain beyond praise. And the great speech of accusation at the trial, played against silence, shot in one immense sustained take lasting most of a reel, justly earned him, and the studio, the respect of the world.

Also in 1936, Dieterle directed *White Angel*, a biography of Florence Nightingale, beautifully written by Mordaunt Shairp, photographed by Tony Gaudio, designed by Anton Grot. Aside from Kay Francis' most sensitive and considered performance of the title role—tender, discreet, perfectly in period—the film marvelously hit off the correct flavor of the Victorian age, particularly in the scenes at the Scutari Hospital in the Crimea, in which director, cameraman and above all set designer were seen at their peak. This noble and compassionate film, flawed though it may have been by some historical inaccuracies, further established the significance of Warners as an organ of serious ideas. Just as in *The Life of Louis Pasteur* rearguard medical attitudes were exposed, and as in *Zola*, the futility and corrpution of military regimes and anti-Semitism (a very indirect attack on Hitler's Germany) were revealed, so *White Angel* showed the stupidity of the officials who prevented Florence Nightingale from doing her proper work. Though today films of this caliber may perhaps seem too consciously "improving" and awkwardly lofty in their sentiments, in the 1930s they were of the utmost value in keeping alive the conscience of a people.

Two other biographies of note were made at the time. These were *The Great Garrick*, directed by James Whale, and starring Brian Aherne, and *The Lady with Red Hair*, based on the life of the actress Mrs. Leslie Carter, directed by Curtis Bernhardt and starring Miriam Hopkins. The first of these two films was originally to have been directed by Mervyn LeRoy, who emerged as producer only. Leroy wrote extensive articles in *The New York Times* discussing the film, for which he and Herman Lissauer prepared extraordinary general research. LeRoy supervised Anton Grot in building a richly authentic set of the Comédie Française. Photographs of the exterior of the theatre and minutely detailed prints of the interiors served as guides. The Theatre Royal in Drury Lane, cradle of Garrick's career, was copied from material supplied by the Victoria and Albert Museum in London. Historic playbills were drawn from. The makeup was scrupulously accurate, and the wigs were made in England.

Mr. Aherne's performance and James Whale's direction were ideally in period. For *The Lady with Red Hair*, another exhaustive research was undertaken by Herman Lissauer. Claude Rains played David Belasco with a suitable flourish, hitting off his shock hair, his clerical collar, and his baggy black clothes to a fault. Miriam Hopkins, though scarcely convincing as a supreme beauty of the stage in the early twentieth century, acted with all the temperament and flair the part called for.

In 1939, the Warners bought a story idea from a writer named Norman Burnside: an account of the career of Dr. Paul Ehrlich, and his battle against syphilis. Developed as *Dr. Ehrlich's Magic Bullet*, the film was directed by Dieterle and co-written by John Huston, Heinz Herald and Burnside himself from letters, clippings, and notes preserved by the doctor's widow, Hedwig, in Switzerland, and by his secretary, Martha Marquardt, in London. Carl Jules Weyl as art director efficiently recreated the Kaiser Wilhelm Hospital, the Koch Institute in Berlin, and the Ehrlich Institute and Georg Speyer Haus in Frankfurt. Sig Rumann, who played Dr. Hans Wolfert, was himself a scientist, working at the time with Dr. Carl Lindegren, professor of bacteriology of the University of Southern California. Three doctors acted as technical advisers, their names, because of professional ethics, removed from the titles. The film was another highly serious, somewhat stately addition to the genre, valuable for its portrayal of medical ethics.

Perhaps the most elaborate picture of the cycle, also made in 1939, was *Juarez*, based by John Huston, Aeneas Mackenzie and Wolfgang Reinhardt on the play *Juarez and Maximilian*, by Franz Werfel, and the book, *The Phantom Crown*, by Bertita Harding. Once again, the classic Warner "prestige" team was assembled: photography by Tony Gaudio, art direction by Anton Grot. Henry Blanke and Hal Wallis produced, Dieterle directed. Plans for the film began as early as 1937, when Herman Lissauer assembled a bibliography of Benito Pablo Juarez, and the tragic story of the Emperor Maximilian and his wife, Carlotta. Lissauer handed Blanke, Dieterle and the writer Aeneas Mackenzie 372 volumes, documents and period photographs, which were given to Paul Muni, cast as Juarez, and to Mackenzie and his fellow writers. Meanwhile, Anton Grot drew 3,643 sketches, from which the engineers prepared 7,360 blueprints for the exteriors and interiors of the castles of Miramon, on the Adriatic Sea, the Tuileries in France, and the Chapultepec Palace in Mexico City. A complete Mexican village was built on the Warner Ranch at Calabasas; L. I. Burns of the wardrobe department outfitted two courts, two armies, and the citizens of 12 villages and four cities; and 54 speaking parts were carefully cast. Muni was a fine Juarez—a slow-speaking, guttural, educated savage—Bette Davis played with great effectiveness the role of the ill-fated Carlotta, and Brian Aherne was ideal as the handsome, refined and absurd Maximilian von Hapsburg.

It was in the prestige cycle that the great Italian cameraman Tony Gaudio and his pupil, Sol Polito, first worked out the richly textured lighting pattern which became a trademark of Warners in the years to come. In the crime films, and even in the musicals, the lighting had been flat, stark, with a grainy, unglossy surface; but, following Hal Mohr's specialized lighting in A *Midsummer Night's Dream*, the studio "look" became increasingly handsome. It depended, of course, chiefly on the films being made virtually in their entirely in the studio: the silent film tradition of *plein air* photography was in the discard, even for such outdoor subjects as *Captain Blood*. The new method was called by Gaudio "precision lighting": Gaudio dispensed with the floodlighting preferred by such men as Barney ("Chick") McGill, replacing it with spotlight beams, each one of which could be meticulously controlled. Like Hal Mohr, Gaudio believed that since all light fell from above, whether sunlight, moonlight, or artificial light, he should arrange his spotlights exclusively on lamprails above the sets. He also used dimmers—four to half a dozen of which were at all times retained by his crew. This meant that he could constantly vary the intensity of light.

On *The Life of Emile Zola*, he was faced with a particularly important problem: lighting an artist's studio designed by Anton Grot with walls which were only five feet high, melding at their apex into a complex series of skylights. Since all of the light would have come from the skylights, casting the walls into black shadows, Gaudio placed a bank of spotlights over the skylight glass, with diffusers casting a faint glow on the opposite rail to relieve the shadows from the keylight and prevent the scene from becoming merely a silhouette.

For part of the scene Paul Muni played with his back to the camera; then he turned facing the camera to speak an important line. Gaudio's lighting balance was no longer dramatically correct, for while the semi-silhouetted effect reproduced what the eye would naturally see, it was dramatically necessary to follow the actor's facial expressions. Gaudio used a small dimmer, connected only to those lamps focused on Muni. Normally, these lamps were dimmed. As Muni started to turn, the dimmer slowly brought the intensity of these lamps up to the correct level. When he turned away, the lamps were dimmed once more.

In *White Angel*, as Florence Nightingale passed through the hospital ward with her lamp in the Crimea, the light on her at each stopping point changed in intensity, the changes caused by an almost incredibly ingenious use of "Gaudio dimmers."

Despite his disastrous work on *A Midsummer Night's Dream*, the cycle also furthered the reputation of the marvelously talented Polish art director Anton Grot, whose deliberately exaggerated Germanic sets fitted the mood of Dieterle's sombre direction. Grot had first come to prominence with his work on Archie Mayo's *Svengali* in 1931, a masterpiece of bizarre foreshortened set design, influenced by German models. Later, his sets for *The Mystery of the Wax Museum* developed, in the two-color system, his theories of expressionist set construction. More creatively involved in his films than the equivalent set directors Hans Dreier at Paramount and Cedric Gibbons at Metro-Goldwyn-Mayer, he could range all the way from the dream-like surrealistic sets of *Gold Diggers of 1933* to the intricate San Franciscan Chinatown of William Wellman's film of the Tong wars, *Hatchet Man;* at all times he worked with a free imagination, deliberately departing from "realism." A master of illusion, he created a world: he even painted in shadows, or superimposed special imitation ceilings to cause patterns of shadows to fall on the walls.

Film music, too, came to be of paramount importance in the prestige cycle, putting Warners firmly ahead of the field in Hollywood. In the mid-1930s, the composers Max Steiner and Erich Wolfgang Korngold arrived at Warners. At RKO-Radio Pictures, Steiner had established a reputation as a pioneer in the dramatic use of music. His score for *King Kong,* in particular, interested some serious critics, and his skilled compositions for *The Lost Patrol* and *The Informer* were not ignored.

Steiner worked to a pattern then common. When a picture was completed and cut, he put the film through a measuring machine and had a cue sheet prepared which gave the exact timing of particular actions and lines of dialogue. Steiner wrote in a book entitled *We Make the Movies* (edited by Nancy Naumberg, W. W. Norton and Company, 1937): "The first two minutes on my imaginary cue sheet consist of the arrival of a train in some little town. I would use music that conforms with the pounding of the locomotive, a train whistle, or the screeching of the brakes, and perhaps some gay music to cover the greetings of people getting on and off the train."

Steiner's music was lilting, romantic, dashing. Korngold's music was more stately, more grandiose and more orchestrally inventive and striking. He was a gifted composer of operas and symphonies, whose works had been conducted by Klemperer and Ormandy. In 1935 he was imported from Vienna, where he had been working on the completion of an opera, *Katrine;* when production was postponed due to the unavailability of the star, Richard Tauber, and the conductor, Bruno Walter, and the directors of the State Opera House announced that they would not proceed without these two men, Korngold angrily snatched up a letter from Warner Brothers offering him a job and accepted it, thus escaping the Nazi incursion into Vienna. His first assignment was to arrange the Mendelssohn music for *A Midsummer Night's Dream*.

Whereas Steiner worked with cue sheets, Korngold emphatically did not. He preferred to work in a private projection room while he improvised the scores on the piano. At home, he developed the music, then returned and with the aid of the projectionist had holes made in the film, which flashed, giving him the correct signals for starting an accompaniment.

Although the style of both Steiner and Korngold is somewhat dated today, they helped many a dull or halting script over dramatic hurdles, carrying the audience along on an engulfing tide of sound. An electricity was set up between screen and public which otherwise might not have existed.

Alongside the biography cycle were the epic films which made Warners immense sums of money in the Depression: stories of high adventure, of cloak and sword and dagger, of billowing sail and rolling sea, of attacks on pirate forts and of good men and true pitted against beetle-browed villains on the Spanish main. Luckily, just as the demand arose for this type of production, the Warners found the right man at the right time: the dashing Irish-Australian, Errol Flynn. Handsome, self-destructive, devil-may-care, he was ideally cast in these sea and land adventures.

Jack Warner can be credited with having seen Errol Flynn's qualities at the outset. Spotting him in an obscure English film entitled *Murder at Monte Carlo*, he imported him to Hollywood at a salary of $150 a week. When Robert Donat, who had been assigned an historical adventure, *Captain Blood*, became unavailable, Jack Warner (in part persuaded by Hal Wallis' sister, Errol

Flynn's agent Minna Wallis) took a gamble and engaged Flynn as a replacement. He had already become fascinated by Flynn, who reminded him of John Barrymore, a hard-drinking, wenching, lovable and handsome man who was in many ways everything Jack Warner himself would like to have been.

Unfortunately, it seemed at first that the gamble on the new man would not pay off. Flynn was nervous, amateurish and clumsy with a sword despite the careful training of the fencing instructor, Fred Cavens. He was unpunctual and undisciplined, and somewhat despised his own appearance on the screen. He fought constantly with the director, Curtiz, who was overbearing and sadistic. Curtiz threw up his hands in despair several times and indeed several early scenes had to be reshot to cover Flynn's inadequacies, with stuntmen doubling in the duals.

It was typical of Warners that they should choose as their next vehicle for Flynn, material which was in the public domain: they did not intend paying authors large sums of money every time they decided to prepare a new "historical" feature. When two writers, Michel Jacoby and Rowland Leigh, brought Jack Warner the idea of basing a film on Tennyson's *The Charge of the Light Brigade,* he was delighted by the notion, and the poem was even printed over the scenes of the charge itself. Jacoby and Leigh traced the history of the British regiments serving in the Crimea to India, where they laid most of the action; thereafter they abandoned history for a complex plot in which a Russian official is shown assisting in an Indian rebellion, and in which two brothers, played by Flynn and Patric Knowles, are in love with the same girl (Olivia de Havilland). Despite the implausible story and the stilted dialogue, the film was a great success in its genre, thanks to the vigor and force of Curtiz' direction and the virtuosity of Sol Polito's camera work.

The preparations for *The Charge of the Light Brigade*

were elaborate, and widely publicized: actual postage stamps of the period were used, in spite of the fact that they would be virtually invisible to the audience, and the uniforms were those originally worn by the 27th Dragoons. When the screenplay was sent to the Warner Brothers' British studio for comment, the executives there firmly rejected the material and instead sent a more accurate screenplay to Hollywood. Hal Wallis was very annoyed at this development; only one idea in the British script was used: the charge was no longer shown to be the climax of the Crimean War, but was instead shown to be linked to the fall of Sebastapol.

The location chosen for the scene of the charge was near Sonora, a valley which resembled the topography of the Crimea. On the north side were hills not unlike the Fedioukines, while on the south and east were elevations not unlike the Causeway Heights. But once again, after so carefully choosing an appropriate setting, the studio rejected accuracy by changing the whole motivation of the charge. Historically, Lord Raglan had directed the Light Brigade to move on Causeway Heights in order to rescue some British cannon. Due to a misinterpretation of the order, a charge was made through the valley, and the force was decimated. In this version, the charge was an act of reckless bravery by Errol Flynn's Captain Durrance.

The scenes of the regiment's crossing of the Khyber Pass were shot in the High Sierras, in conditions of intense cold and howling wind. Patric Knowles, who had been rushed in for the part of Errol Flynn's brother, arrived from London after a severe Atlantic crossing, ill, exhausted and pale, and following a hasty fitting at Western Costumes.

At the outset of the first scene in which he appeared with Flynn, Curtiz yelled out characteristically, "OK, Knowles, ACT!" Knowles, who had never been astride a horse before, promptly fell off. He learned, after numerous knocks, to ride, but whole scenes were postponed while he painfully mastered the art.

From the cold of the Sierras, the location shifted to Chatsworth near Los Angeles where the siege of the Indian fortress of Chukoti was staged. Here the heat was as intense as the cold had been in the mountains; nobody could sleep comfortably at night, and the heavy tan makeup, greasy and uncomfortable, trickled down the impeccably starched white uniforms, ruining them. In many shots in the finished film, the acute observer could see where the makeup was left slightly above the collar line.

During the scenes of the charge itself Curtiz lived up to his terrible reputation for causing injuries to animals: horse after horse tumbled on the tripwires, their limbs so severely maimed they had to be shot, and the S.P.C.A. complained violently.

Flynn's next film, *The Adventures of Robin Hood*, suspensefully written by Seton I. Miller and Norman Reilly Raine in a style which rejected period fustian, was a light entertainment. Here the Warners flair for the action film, the historical film and the "prestige picture" came together with thrilling effect. The direction was begun by William Keighley, replaced early in the shooting by Michael Curtiz, when the rushes proved unsatisfactory to both the producer Henry Blanke and the writer. Curtiz' hand is certainly predominant, the virility of the action scenes and the sense of history unerring as always. Tony Gaudio and Sol Polito provided the finest photography yet to emerge from the studio, a vindication of the comparatively new three color Technicolor system. With its muted greens and browns and vivid touches of scarlet, the film had the look of an illuminated manuscript, and Milo Anderson's costumes had a marvelous authenticity. Errol Flynn remained for a generation of children the only possible Robin Hood: dressed in Sherwood green, always laughing, a feather in his cap, he was charming, dashing and courageous: the finest screen hero of them all. And the film, launched with an inspired publicity campaign which included the issuing of a parchment Sherwood Forest Gazette and numerous study guides to the script for the aid of school children, was an immediate success and firmly established Flynn as a major star.

Making *The Adventures of Robin Hood* was not an inconsiderable task. Shooting began on September 26, 1937, and was finished on January 14, 1938—a far cry from Warners' old, rushed schedules. Four hundred people were sent north to Bidwell Park Forest near Chico, and Richardson Springs, California, with scores of stunt men whose total bill came to $100,000. Twenty thousand properties were manufactured including bows, arrows, crossbows, broadswords, battle axes, maces, pennant standards, armor, and caparisons for the horses. For the scenes in Nottingham Castle, a magnificent creation of the art director Carl Jules Weyl, 270 sun arcs were manned by 90 electricians. For Sir Guy of Gisbourne's banquet, the studio made 500 pieces of period brass: 18 platters 30 inches in circumference held the boars' heads, pigs, sides of venison, pheasant and game fowl. There were horn goblets of spun brass, and 110 brass tankards each holding half a gallon of real wine. The lighting was provided by six huge torchères 14 feet high and weighing half a ton, each bearing 64 flames. Twelve wall cassettes each seven feet long by seven feet high held twelve flambeaux.

The cast had a wonderful time at Chico, shooting trout with bow and arrow, killing wild boar, and swimming in the forest streams—living out the glorious adventure of the film in reality. Eugene Pallette who played Friar Tuck would prepare wonderful feasts at night for everyone, and the feeling of camaraderie was very intense. In breaks in the shooting or on weekends, Patric Knowles, who played Will Scarlett, would take Errol Flynn on joy flights in a small plane; after only one or two sketchy lessons, Flynn insisted upon taking to the air as a pilot himself, causing the studio, and particularly the insurance men, extreme distress. Later, when matching scenes were done at Sherwood Lake and Forest near Los Angeles, Flynn would sail away on his yacht from San Pedro on weekends with Knowles and other cronies, and frequently send the yacht careening close to rocks or other boats in order to terrify members of the expedition. His self-destructive leanings would have driven him to perform his own stunts as well, if the studio had not insisted upon a stunt man double—jumping out of trees onto passing members of the cavalry, taking an arrow firmly on the chest, and grappling head-on with members of King John's foot soldiers.

For *The Adventures of Robin Hood,* Erich Wolfgang Korngold devised the most intricate score composed in Hollywood up to that time. Tossing aside the 600-page file brought to him by the research department on 12th century music, he began work on his own operatic themes, providing in seven weeks 257 pages of sketches, 2,788 bars and 47 themes, running the length of a full symphonic score. Like Max Steiner, he believed in "Mickey Mousing," that is to say, using a melody for each of the characters and situations in turn. When Robin Hood and Sir Guy of Gisbourne clashed for the first time, their themes were interwoven or used in violent counterpoint. When Robin Hood and his Merry Men set out in Sherwood Forest, Korngold supplied a somewhat heated and reckless march theme. Maid Marian was accompanied by a delicate phrase on the strings, suggestive of her fragility and charm; King Richard was announced by a noble *maestoso.* Friar Tuck was introduced by a *religioso* with a *berceuse* interlaced with bassoons suggesting his snores as he slept. The "love theme"—love themes or *leitmotifs* were prime features of 1930s film music—accompanying the romantic involvement of Robin Hood and Maid

Marian was a 3/4 time *andante expressif* played with rich and swelling strings at the finale. Moreover, Korngold worked very closely with the editor, Ralph Dawson, and the sound department under Nathan Levinson and George R. Groves on the extraordinarily complex tournament scene. The fanfare of trumpets at the outset, the twanging of the bowstrings and thud of the arrows, the clash of armor and the swelling *marche galante* accompanying the arrival of the mounted warriors were mixed and scored with a martial flourish and splendor.

The film was released to an overwhelmingly enthusiastic public in late 1938. But the historians were outraged, and many hundreds of letters arrived from both American and British specialists complaining of the errors in the film. Details of the clothing of Robin Hood, King John, and Friar Tuck were condemned outright in newspaper and magazine articles on both sides of the Atlantic. Over 500 letters complained about the appearance of the crosses on the chests of King Richard I and his Holy Crusaders upon their return from the Middle East; the authors of the letters pointed out that the knights of the Crusades wore crosses on their chests while leaving for the Holy Land, and on their backs upon their return. The printed reply sent to all complainants was: "We appreciate your complaint. But it was dramatically necessary for Richard to reveal the cross in front of Robin by throwing open his monk's disguise after he returned and met the Merry Men. It would have been awkward for him to have to turn around while his attendants lifted the cloak and pointed out the mystic symbol."

The next major film in the cycle of adventure films was *The Private Lives of Elizabeth and Essex* (1939) based on Maxwell Anderson's play *Elizabeth the Queen* by Norman Reilly Raine and Aeneas MacKenzie. It was sumptuously photographed in color by Sol Polito, scored by Korngold, and designed to perfection by Grot. Bette

Davis played the Queen with great flair, attack and an agreeably acid edge; Errol Flynn, though essentially miscast as the Earl of Essex, looked handsome and played with dash and skill in the rich satins and silks of Orry-Kelly's costumes. Unhappily, the script was labored and pedantic, Michael Curtiz' direction uncharacteristically stiff, of an almost Dieterle-like heaviness, and the endless confrontations, intrigues and stand-up quarrels of Queen Elizabeth's court became excessively vexing ordeals. It was clear that much of the vitality which had animated *Captain Blood* and *The Adventures of Robin Hood* was beginning to run out. The film was originally entitled *The Lady and the Knight*, until Bette Davis objected that "a Queen is not a lady."

The last of the series of epics starring Errol Flynn was *The Sea Hawk*, based on Seton I. Miller's script about the freebooters of the Spanish Main. Errol Flynn played Geoffrey Thorpe, an itinerant seaman of the court of Queen Elizabeth, played on this occasion by Flora Robson.

For *The Sea Hawk*, Anton Grot devised the "Warner Ocean"—the largest tank yet used in Hollywood—covering an entire sound stage some 30 feet deep, containing a Spanish galleon 136 feet long and a British man-of-war of almost the same size, with a six hundred foot back projection of waves and sky. In some scenes, a door was rolled up so that the tanks could be linked to the Warner Lake, an artificial pool outside. The ships were fixed on hydraulic rockers set at the base of the tank, and the sets were hinged to give the illusion of a vessel rolling at sea; wind machines were used to whip up waves. A special device created an effect of ripples in the water and formations of cirrus or cumulus clouds in the sky.

As always, the director Curtiz drove the cast and crew pitilessly. In a scene of the whipping of the galley slaves, David Kashner, a specialist in whipping who had flicked a

127

rose from Dorothy Lamour's lips in *The Road to Singapore* and had performed several stunts in *Union Pacific*, had to be seen lashing the bare back of Errol Flynn. Curtiz kept saying to him: "Lay it on. Don't be timid. Flynn may be a star outside but here he is only a slave." Kashner evidently took Curtiz seriously; the whip knocked Flynn's wig off and cut him stingingly across his ear. Flynn rose up and flew at the man; and it took three extras to prevent him from beating up both Kashner and Curtiz.

Overlong and overly elaborate, *The Sea Hawk* had a mixed reception. By the outset of the 1940s the public interest in adventure films and solid historical biographies began to run out. A significant event took place on July 28, 1940: the studio dissolved the contracts of Paul Muni and William Dieterle simultaneously, the official reason being that Warners did not have enough money to make prestige pictures; actually, Muni's tantrums and excessive demands had aggravated Hal Wallis and Jack Warner beyond endurance. When he refused to play the leading role in a gangster melodrama, *High Sierrra*, unless the script was rewritten without any gunplay, it was the last straw. His rewriting of much of *Juarez* to emphasize his own role had already, Hal Wallis felt, damaged the picture, which turned out to be a commercial failure. *We Are Not Alone*, a harrowing drama set in an English seaport, with Muni cast as a murderer had also proven to be a disaster at the box office. It was obvious that Muni was through.

Everyone had had enough of Dieterle's high-handedness. His long sojourn at the studio was endured only because of the box office success of his earlier films. The Warners had wearied also of his ponderous, clumsy approach to scenes. Only six months earlier, Dieterle had offered to buy out his contract for $50,000; now, he was released without settlement. It was the end of an era. But the biography cycle did continue sporadically throughout the decade, with lives of Mark Twain and the Brontë sisters.

Social Realism

During the period of the rise of the prestige picture and the epic of adventure, the history of Warners was never free of trouble. On the screen, the studio may have exuded bravado and gusto, but in Hollywood the tensions had never really relaxed. In May, 1934, all of the films of Warner Brothers, Vitaphone and First National were prohibited in Poland, the Minister of the Interior stating that in several crime films "Polacks" were portrayed as vicious hoodlums. In *The Life of Jimmy Dolan,* as an example, a vicious prize fighter and criminal was called Pulaski, the name of a Polish national hero, Count Casimir Pulaski; and they claimed that there was criticism of Poland in *The Match King,* a biography of the swindler Ivar Kreuger.

On August 28 of that year, Mrs. Benjamin Warner,

mother of the brothers, died of a cerebral hemorrhage at the age of 76, with Jack Warner and his sister Sadie at her bedside.

On December 5, 1934, a fire started in a machine shop where repairs were being made on various stage properties. Fanned by a violent Santa Ana wind, the flames spread to a property warehouse and snapped up more than $100,000 worth of oriental rugs and European and American antiques, moving on to five scene docks, the plumbing shop, the pattern shop, a garage and truck shed, a $10,000 camera boom, the replating plant, the sandblasting shop and many of the early Vitagraph films and Vitagraph, First National and Warner correspondence and production records. Bing Crosby and Dick Powell, Sally Eilers and Helen Morgan saw the smoke and flames from their homes in Toluca Lake not far away; while the men helped as volunteer fire fighters, the ladies served hot coffee to the firemen. The fire broke out just as Michael Curtiz was shooting the last sequence of *Black Fury,* with Paul Muni, and Curtiz and 65 extras playing coal miners joined in the fire fighting. One set fell down, injuring the actor Raymond Hoop, several employees suffered from burns and crushed limbs, and Albert M. Rounder, chief of the studio fire department, collapsed with a fatal heart attack just after the blaze was brought under control.

Nor were the brothers' troubles over after that. In January, 1935, they faced an anti-trust case in St. Louis; they were charged with having attempted to acquire a monopoly of theatres in the area, and refusing to supply films to theatres not under their ownership. On February 1, in the Federal District Court of Philadelphia, Judge Walsh absolutely forbade Warners—and the other movie companies—to force exhibitors to show their products, or to refuse them these products if they were under independent management and wished to make bookings.

On April 27, 1935, the brothers were again in court,

when in New York, Harry Armstrong and Richard H. Gerard, composer and author of the song "Sweet Adeline" used in Mervyn LeRoy's film of that title, brought suit against the brothers for $250,000, and against the music publishers M. Witmark and Company, claiming that they had written the song some 30 years earlier and that they were supposed to receive 33⅓ percent of all royalties received for its performance. They said that Witmark and Warner Brothers had made an agreement without consulting or compensating them: the case was settled out of court.

In September, 1935, a theatre restaurant owner in New York, Edward Hutchison, also sued the brothers, claiming that he was all too clearly represented in the Al Jolson film *Go into Your Dance,* represented as a "racketeer, thug, murderer and promoter of illegal, immoral and criminal enterprises." This case, too, was settled out of court.

In November, Benjamin Warner followed his wife into death. He had been visiting his daughter, Mrs. David Robins, in Youngstown, Ohio, when he was stricken. He was buried in Los Angeles on November 9, beside his wife and Sam. A few days later, the brothers learned that they had been acquitted of all charges of monopolizing in the St. Louis suit.

On January 11, 1936, Jack Warner married for the second time, his marriage with Irma Warner having been dissolved several years earlier. His new bride, Ann, was the former wife of the silent film star, Don Alvarado; it proved to be a happy marriage and Ann a brilliant hostess. But Warner's joy was short-lived: that year the worst battle he had ever experienced with a star vexed him beyond endurance: it was his struggle with the up-and-coming young actress Bette Davis.

In the past years, Bette Davis had become the studio's chief portrayer of vicious or wronged women in a series of soap operas put together with a great deal of commercial skill and very little of the artistic merit which distinguished the studio's efforts in the field of social realism. Almost invariably, it was the tough realistic bite of Miss Davis' performances which saved her vehicles from becoming intolerably maudlin. In Archie Mayo's *Bordertown*, the first of the series following Miss Davis' successful appearance on loan to RKO-Radio for *Of Human Bondage*, she argued constantly with the director, Archie Mayo, to ensure more accuracy in her playing: in one scene, he wanted her to sit up in bed in the morning with a perfectly made up face and an impeccable coiffure, and she insisted upon wearing face cream and tousling her hair.

Her first major women's picture directed by Alfred E. Green was *Dangerous*, written from his own story—based on the career of Jeanne Eagels, an actress who fascinated Miss Davis—by Laird Doyle, photographed by Ernest Haller. The script was a mélange of dramatic cliches about an actress fallen on bad ways who is redeemed by the love of a good architect; when the architect, played by Franchot Tone, is crippled in a car accident which she herself caused, she selflessly devotes herself to him for life. It was with great difficulty that Miss Davis—all saucer eyes, flapping arms and broken voice—managed to create a rounded character from this novelette. Her sheer energy made the acting of the maudlin situations watchable; it earned her an Oscar. And she managed, by sheer force of talent, to turn Robert Sherwood's pretentious, "literary" play *The Petrified Forest* into a woman's picture: her own. Produced by Henry Blanke, directed by Archie Mayo from a script by Charles Kenyon and Delmer Daves, photographed by Sol Polito, the film succeeded in re-creating the arid heat of Arizona, the seedy atmosphere of a roadside service station. Above all, though, the film made a star of Humphrey Bogart, perfect as the snarling gangster Duke Mantee, and it confirmed once and for all Miss Davis' greatness. Speaking in an oddly high-pitched, nervous voice, her face pinched and drawn, she played the uneasily ambitious painter Gabby Maple with extraordinary intensity. Because of the quality of her acting, and that of the frustrated society wife by Genevieve Tobin, the film captivated an immense audience of women.

Unfortunately, after the great success of this film, Miss Davis was wasted on worthless pictures, beginning with Alfred E. Green's lamentable *Golden Arrow* and a travesty of *The Maltese Falcon, Satan Met a Lady.* As a result of her dissatisfaction with this last production, Miss Davis walked out of the studio and signed a contract with Ludovic Toeplitz, a producer of prestige pictures in England. She sailed across the Atlantic on the *Duchess of Bedford* and embarked upon an extended tour of the country with her husband, Harmon Nelson. Meanwhile, Jack Warner arranged a meeting with Toeplitz in Venice, and succeeded in obtaining an injunction restraining her from employment until such time as she would appear in court.

The Bette Davis case began before Mr. Justice Branson in the King's Bench Division of the High Court of Chancery on October 14, 1936. Bette Davis' defense was that Warners had forced her in breach of contract to play unsuitable roles, and had required her again in breach of contract to work over 14 hours a day. In view of these breaches, she was in a position to offer her services elsewhere, and the contract was no longer valid. Sir Patrick Hastings, KC, Norman Birkett, KC, and Frank Gahan appeared for Warner Brothers, and Sir William Jowitt, KC, J. D. Cassels, KC, and J.L.S. Hale appeared for Miss Davis.

Hastings, in a witty and cleverly argued opening for

the plaintiffs, made great play with the fact that Miss
Davis was receiving $3000 a week, that Clause Nine of
her contract expressly forbade her to appear under any
other aegis, and that she had acted in breach of contract
by not appearing on June 19, 1936, as specifically requested, for the picture *God's Country and the Woman.*
She had refused by telegram on June 18. Jack Warner
then appeared on the witness stand. He pointed out that
his company had promoted Miss Davis from obscurity
to a very great height in her profession, and that her
films were grossing between $600,000 to $700,000 round
the world. He had not been aware of complaints from her,
and one of the vehicles prepared for her, *Dangerous,* had
won her an Oscar.

The hearing continued on October 15, through October 20. Alexander Korda, the English producer, supported
Warner's evidence. Sir William Jowitt, acting for Miss
Davis, analyzed the contract, showing how completely it
bound the star hand and foot for working schedules and
public appearances; Sir Patrick caused great amusement
by saying that "slavery at $3000 a week was a slavery to
which very few people would object." During the hearing, Gerald Gardiner, acting for Toeplitz, continued to object to Sir Patrick's statements that Toeplitz had "bribed"
Miss Davis to appear in his films.

On October 19, Mr. Justice Branson gave his sum-
ming-up and judgment. He summarized once again the
contract, which was "extremely stringent," and in which
Miss Davis agreed "to render her exclusive services as a
motion picture and legitimate stage actress" to the plaintiffs, and that she would not work for anybody else. He
said that in his view only the desire for more money had
prompted her to break her contract illegally and go to England for her contract with Toeplitz. After citing a number
of cases of severance of agreements, Branson found for
the plaintiffs.

It was a triumph for Jack Warner. He acted mag-
nanimously by paying up Miss Davis' costs and preparing
better scripts for her, beginning with Seton I. Miller's admirable scenario for *Marked Woman,* a story of Lucky
Luciano's prostitution rackets, capably directed by Lloyd
Bacon, but it was not until she made *Jezebel* in 1938 about
a tempestuous Southern belle that the star again emerged
in a major film. For the first time she worked under the direction of an important figure: William Wyler. She wrote
in her memoirs, *The Lonely Life* (G. P. Putnam's Sons,
1962): "It was Wyler who helped me realize my full potential as an actress. I met my match in this exceptionally
creative and talented director." It was chiefly a question
for Wyler of controlling Miss Davis' overcharged, exhausting delivery of lines; he disciplined her energy, forcing
her to avoid a baroque approach, to seek out the truth of a
character. He compelled her to make every gesture count;
hitherto, she had been wasteful of gesture. When she entered a set for the first time, passionate, determined, in a
hunting habit, he made her play the scene over and over
again so that her energy was reduced. The novelettish
scene in which the sluttish Julie shocks everyone by
wearing a red dress to a ball was given a great deal of
depth by Wyler's scrupulous handling.

Unfortunately, Miss Davis' next film, *The Sisters,* was
much less satisfactory, a labored story about three sisters
in San Francisco, with a perfunctory 1906 earthquake introduced to heighten the drama. For *Dark Victory,* made
in 1938, Jack Warner did her far more proud: he engaged
two of the men chiefly responsible for the woman's picture at MGM, the producer David Lewis and the director
Edmond Goulding. Both men were sophisticated, subtle,
careful in handling women stars, and they had a specialized knowledge of period costumes, hair styles and makeup. Together, they brought a new elegance and quietness
of tone to the hitherto rowdy Warner ambience. From

their arrival may be traced the steady increase of softness, romantic warmth and generosity in the Warner films, which blossomed most notably in the 1940s; and Bette Davis responded fully to their guidance.

Dark Victory also began Miss Davis' important association with the accomplished screenwriter Casey Robinson. The story was based very loosely on a failed Broadway play for Tallulah Bankhead, written by George Emerson Brewer, Jr., and Bertram Block. It was in essence pure soap: a frivolous heiress is stricken with a brain disease and gradually goes blind. Yet the careful direction, the scrupulous precision of the medical details—a result of David Lewis' and Casey Robinson's careful consulting with experts at the Cedars of Lebanon Hospital— and most importantly Miss Davis' controlled, quietly anguished playing, made the film a compelling work. Her only difference with both producer and director was in the matter of the acting of the penultimate scene, shot at Malibu Lake. In this sequence, which became famous, the heiress Judith Traherne is planting hyacinth seeds in a garden with her friend Ann King, played by Geraldine Fitzgerald, when she senses the onset of blindness. She feels the heat on her hand, but her failing eyes sense that the sun has gone behind a cloud, a very effective dramatic invention of Robinson's. Miss Davis wanted to play the scene nobly, happily; but Lewis insisted that she should show a moment of panic. "No one wants to die," he told her. The words gave her a new insight into the character, making her final bravery in facing death seem more effectively moving.

Dark Victory was a great success for everyone connected with it. Bette Davis again appeared under the direction of Goulding and in a Casey Robinson screenplay in *The Old Maid,* based on the novel by Edith Wharton. The period of Civil War and its aftermath was carefully re-created by the art director, Robert Haas, and by the costume designer, Orry-Kelly: Gaudio's lighting was somberly beautiful: and the tender playing of Miss Davis, pitted against the more obvious theatrics of her co-star, Miriam Hopkins, once more showed that Goulding had the ability to obtain the best from her. She proved, if proof still were needed, that she was, together with Garbo, the finest actress in Hollywood; capable of suggesting vulnerability, pain, and personal distress better than almost anyone else.

During the middle and late 1930s, the studio had not relinquished its leading position as a fount of vigorous social comment, carefully analyzing the flaws in American society. Indeed, one of the finest films of the period, Mervyn LeRoy's film *They Won't Forget* (1937) based on Ward Green's book *Death in the Deep South* by Aben Kandel and Robert Rossen, remains one of the most important of all of Hollywood's exposes of racial prejudice. Now that, through the pioneer work of Hal Mohr, Tony Gaudio and Sol Polito, the appearance of the studio's films had become much richer, its lighting style more striking and complex, and the studio's new financial wealth permitted a more expansive, less rushed approach to a subject, a film of this kind no longer resembled a tabloid newspaper article. In every respect, *They Won't Forget* was a considerable advance on such pioneer works as the same director's *I Am a Fugitive from a Chain Gang*. Arthur Edeson's photography was firmly in the Mohr-Gaudio-Polito tradition of "precision lighting," supported by Robert Haas' discreetly Anton Grot-like art direction, copied from the offices, streets and courtroom interiors of small Southern towns. In this story of a black janitor accused of murdering a white girl (played by the young Lana Turner), the script was full of vivid, pointed detail, and the playing was excellent. Claude Rains' bigoted lawyer, and Allyn Joslyn's unscrupulous crime reporter both provided classic portrayals of vindictiveness.

Almost as important, and equally in the correct tradition, *Bullets or Ballots* (1936) skillfully written by Seton I. Miller and directed by William Keighley, owed a great deal to *The March of Time* series of documentaries, beginning with a Westbrook Van Voorhis-like voice, the camera focusing on a spinning globe of the world. The film was a natural successor to *Five Star Final*, but without the sentimentality which disfigured that film: it was based on the reminiscences of a New York reporter, Martin Mooney, and offered a strong portrait of Dutch Schultz, thinly disguised as "Al Kreuger," played by Barton MacLane. Hal Mohr's photography exemplified his own precision lighting principles and a scrupulous addiction to natural light sources. Edward G. Robinson, as the character based on Martin Mooney, was remarkably good. In the same manner, *Black Legion*, written for Archie Mayo by Aben Finkel, William Wister Haines and Robert Lord piercingly analyzed the evils of the Ku Klux Klan, based on actual events in Detroit, and showed the emergence of Humphrey Bogart from the showy pyrotechnics of *The Petrified Forest* to a more profound and considered acting style. The film underscored the mindlessness of factory workers gradually corrupted by a xenophobic element which condemned the employment of foreign labor, making *Black Legion* a worthy companion piece to Warners' earlier study of labor problems, Michael Curtiz' *Black Fury*.

Early in 1938, Jack Warner got wind of the fact that the Federal Bureau of Investigation had discovered a number of Nazi spies operating in the Eastern states. With the approval of Roosevelt, he decided to send a contract writer, Milton Krims, who had long been pressing to do an anti-Nazi film, to New York to work with the FBI investigator, Leon Turrou. Krims abandoned a scheme to write a contemporary version of *The Captain from Kopenick* and set to work. The idea appealed to him strongly, as he had covered the Munich crisis for *Collier's Magazine,* and he was determined to provide an illustration of the Nazi threat. He also insisted from the outset on a semidocumentary approach.

Hal Wallis and Robert Lord called Krims into the office and told him the film would be made in absolute secrecy. He prepared a massive dossier with Turrou based on numerous meetings of the German-American Bund which he attended, disguised as a Nazi, himself. He also attended the trial of the various spies when they were apprehended, obtaining a complete trial transcript. Returning to Hollywood, and working closely with Turrou, who had a set of photographs of the homes of the chief protagonists, he prepared an extremely factual screenplay. Among those he drew with care in the writing—he used notes on their appearance and bearing at the trial—were Dr. Ignatz T. Griebl, Gustav Rumrich, Johanna Hoffman, Mrs. Kate Moog Busch, and Karl Schluter.

Meanwhile, Turrou published a series of articles on the spies in the New York *Post,* to which Warners obtained the rights. He was dismissed from the FBI by J. Edgar Hoover, who had forbidden him to make capital out of FBI matters or to make use of material from the files. Turrou's manuscript was, of course, initially available to Krims. Hal Wallis, the producer, asked Anatole Litvak to direct, and Edward G. Robinson to star in the role of Turrou. Paul Lukas appeared as Dr. Griebl, Francis Lederer as Rumrich, Dorothy Tree as Johanna Hoffman, Lya Lys as Mrs. Kate Moog Busch, and George Sanders as Schluter. It was an act of extraordinary daring for Warners to have prepared the film at a time when America was still very largely isolationist.

Milton Krims had grave differences with Anatole Litvak, who wanted to open the film with shots of Nazi atrocities, and to introduce elements of melodramatic fiction into the plot. Krims wanted to concentrate on absolute realism. The differences of the two men continued during the shooting, when Litvak used a somewhat heated and kitschy approach to some scenes, while Krims, constantly complaining to Wallis, insisted upon a more subdued and quiet approach.

In the early days of preparation and production, Edward G. Robinson, Lya Lys, and other members of the cast received a number of threatening letters and telegrams demanding that they cease working if they wished to avoid bodily harm.

Georg Gyssling, consul for Germany in Los Angeles, strenuously fought to have the film cancelled. The German government lodged severe complaints with the Diplomatic Department in Washington, and the German chargé d'affaires, Hans Thomsen, delivered a message to Secretary of State Cordell Hull denouncing the picture as an example of "pernicious propaganda poisoning German-American relations." Germany arranged for the film to be banned at once in Italy, Japan, Sweden and Yugoslavia, and Dr. Josef Goebbels' press department in Berlin announced that the German film industry would be preparing retaliatory propaganda films focusing on American gangsterism and judicial corruption, rather overlooking the fact that Warners had been making precisely that kind of picture for several years.

Jack and Ann Warner were threatened with anonymous notes, and the moment the film was released the German-American Bund sued the company for $500,000 damages; * the case was dropped when Fritz Kuhn, for-

---

* In its issue of May 18, 1939, the German-American Bund newspaper said: "The producer of this nightmarish concoction has drawn for his material on the choicest collection of flubdub that a diseased mind could possibly pick out of the public ashcan.

merly head of the Bund, who had joined in the suit, was jailed for appropriating Bund funds for his own use. The German government proceeded to fulfill its earlier threat of banning the production throughout Europe, and the film, entitled *Confessions of a Nazi Spy*, suffered commercially for that reason.

Confessions of a Nazi Spy was a flop in the United States, as the public refused to believe in the events which Krims had portrayed in his script.* Nevertheless, it remained, together with *They Won't Forget*, Warner Brothers' most important document of the period, and today is an invaluable source of reference for social historians.

Confessions of a Nazi Spy was followed immediately in 1940 by *Underground*, directed by Vincent Sherman from Charles Grayson's screenplay—adapting an original story by Edwin Justus Mayer and Oliver H. P. Garrett—a harsh account of dissatisfaction, treachery and poisonous ambition within the Nazi ranks. With striking effectiveness, the film showed the existence of illegal radio stations in Germany, of Nazi German suppression of free thought, of torture and murder of Jews, of spying by servants on their own masters. Minutely researched, the film caused severe criticism from isolationist elements in the community, and was in many ways even more daring, though much less well dramatized than *Confessions of a Nazi Spy*.

Warners' next major propaganda picture, *Dive Bomber*, made in 1940, produced by Robert Lord, was extraordinary in that it was evidently intended as a display of American strength in the Pacific one year before the Japanese attacked Pearl Harbor. Shot at the San Diego Naval Base, which stood in for the Honolulu Naval Base, and using PBY5 Consolidated bombers, interceptors, tor-

---

* Additional dialogue was written by John Wexley during the production, after Krims declined to continue working with Litvak.

pedo bombers, aircraft carrier and dive bombers, the film effectively illustrated not only United States air power in the Pacific but gave the public an insight into the physical problems of dive bombing and of flying in the stratosphere. Through the protagonists, played by Flynn and Fred MacMurray, the public learned about embolisms, blackouts and night blindness—thanks to the extremely well-researched script by Frank Wead and Robert Buckner.

Though not directly related to the war, *Sergeant York*, made shortly before Pearl Harbor in 1941, also confirmed the concern of the studio with patriotic themes. Sergeant Alvin C. York was a man from the Tennessee hill country, deeply religious and conscientious, and devoted to his family, who had answered the call to arms in 1917. Upon his return from service as a hero, he had been offered by Jesse L. Lasky of Famous Players-Lasky a considerable sum to sell his story to the screen as a subject for Cecil B. DeMille. He had declined the offer, and had declined it again in 1930. In 1940, he yielded to the further entreaties of Lasky, who had now joined Warners as a producer, on condition that he should supervise the entire production in detail. He checked every detail of every scene, personally approving the choice of Gary Cooper as star. The film was directed skillfully by Howard Hawks, from a screenplay by Aben Finkel, Harry Chandlee, Howard Koch and John Huston. The reviews for the production were uniformly enthusiastic and the public reception was overwhelming.

11

War!

JUST BEFORE PEARL HAR-
bor, Warners made two very important adaptations of novels. The first was *The Maltese Falcon*, which Henry
Blanke asked John Huston to adapt and direct. Dashiell
Hammett's novel had already supplied the basis for two
previous films at Warners, neither of them successful.

Huston proved to be the ideal man for the job. Laconic, satirical, cool, he was a perfect Warner alumnus.
He and Blanke stuck to the novel closely, pasting up
pages and fitting in camera instructions. The story was a
little dated. It dealt with a group of people who were
looking urgently for a small black statue of a bird said to
have been encrusted with gems by the Knights of Malta
as tribute to the Emperor Charles V. The trick was to
make the material seem contemporary and fresh, and in
this Blanke and Huston succeeded.

They cast carefully. Humphrey Bogart, as wry and dis-illusioned a Warner product as Huston himself, was the right choice for Sam Spade, Hammett's acidly honest de-tective. Huston sneaked Mary Astor, who had been caught up in a scandal, through the back door to play Brigid O'Shaughnessy, the psychotic liar who vamps Sam Spade. The notoriety surrounding her at the time was subtly exploited by the choice. Peter Lorre proved to be well suited to the role of the effeminate Joel Cairo. A new actor, Sydney Greenstreet, who had appeared with the Lunts in *There Shall Be No Night*, made a convincing Gutman, a gross epitome of greed. Huston wisely ar-ranged for the cast to meet each day for lunch near Bur-bank. This ensured a sense of intimacy in their playing. The direction was intensely disciplined, and the film be-came a critical and commercial success.

The other important adaptation of 1941 was Henry Bellaman's *Kings Row*. It was somewhat daring for Warners to make this subject at all, since the novel, a sort of dark reversal of Sinclair Lewis, dealt in corrupt medical practices, sadism and incest in a small town. Casey Robin-son skillfully telescoped the material. Sam Wood was engaged to direct. Since Wood was quite incapable of shaping a film visually, he worked with William Cameron Menzies, a gifted designer, and the great James Wong Howe, whose camera work glossed over faults in the di-rection. The cast did not play uniformly well. Betty Field as the tragic Cassie Towers, Claude Rains as her father, and Ann Sheridan as Randy, the quintessential small town girl, were touching and effective. Robert Cummings as Parris Mitchell, the book's protagonist, a prototype of youthful idealism in the person of a young doctor, was not adequate to the demands of his role. This handicap se-verely weakened the film. The score by Erich Wolfgang Korngold was a distinguished if ponderous accompani-ment. In a scene at the end in which a young man played by Ronald Reagan loses his legs in an accident, Jack Warner told Korngold to provide something "more emotional." "How about the 'Blue Danube'?" Korngold said as he went home to write some new rhapsodic pages.

Warners continued with its program of shorts, including *Service with the Colors* (the Army), *Meet the Fleet, March On, Marines, Wings of Steel* (Army Air Corps), *Here Comes the Cavalry, Soldiers in White* (medical corps), and *The Tanks Are Coming.*

In June, 1941, the studio announced its purchase of Irving Berlin's *This Is the Army*, a Broadway revue with a cast of 300 soldiers, originally prepared for the benefit of the Army Relief Fund. A program of instructional documentaries was prepared at the old Vitagraph Studios in Brooklyn, which had not been used since the time of the first talkies. Each of these was to be sent to troops serving overseas.

Another step in 1941 was the appointment of the casting director, Steve Trilling, as assistant to Jack Warner and after that as head of production. Discreet and able, he proved to have a fine record in the next few years, sustaining a policy of skilled picture-making while unfortunately attracting little or no attention within the industry itself.

In 1942, the feeling at the studio was that war films need not be entirely serious: that an Errol Flynn adventure with a war theme was perfectly acceptable. Ironically, he was rejected for the army because he suffered from syphilis. The writers gradually converted his image into that of a contemporary Robin Hood, battling with the Nazis for the protection of the "little people" of occupied Europe. He suffered from the irony. In *Desperate Journey,* Arthur T. Horman's script had him as Flight Lieutenant Terence Forbes, an Australian member of the crew of an RAF bomber which is shot down in Europe. After a series of daring espionage achievements, Flynn and his crew escape despite the efforts of a Nazi *gauleiter* played by Raymond Massey. The film was aided commercially by the fact that in 1942 Errol Flynn was the accused party in a notorious paternity suit. In 1943, Flynn appeared in *Edge of Darkness*, as Gunner Brogge, a fisherman in charge of the underground in a Norwegian village. In 1944 he was in *Northern Pursuit*, as Steve Wagner, a Canadian Mountie who traps a Nazi insurgent group in Canada. Most notoriously, in 1945, he won the Burma war single-handed in *Objective, Burma!*, a work which was castigated in Great Britain and withdrawn after the first screening at the Warner Theatre in London. These films, directed for the most part by Raoul Walsh, were not good, but they proved of value in keeping Americans interested in the European and Far East conflict.

After Pearl Harbor, Warners quadrupled its output of patriotic shorts under the direction of Gordon Hollingshead and Cedric Francis. Among these films the most important was *Beyond the Line of Duty*, which showed Captain Hewitt T. Wheless tackling 18 Japanese Zero warplanes in *Winning Your Wings*. Lieutenants Ronald Reagan and Burgess Meredith appeared in *Rear Gunner*. Other important shorts were *Commandos of the Skies, Safety in Aviation, I'll Tell You What the Army Air Force Is, Takeoffs and Landings,* and *Thirteen Aces*. A film called *105 HM Howitzer* was made in two sections, the first in 16 reels, the second in eight, and a four-reel *Oxygen in Aviation* proved invaluable. In 1943 the Vitagraph studios in New York were presented free of charge to the Army Air Forces Motion Picture Unit for the duration of the war. Ninety-five percent of Warner employees became subscribers to War Bonds, and $20,000 worth of bonds and stamps were sold at the studio each week. Three hundred employees were in the armed forces, and at home Bette Davis and John Garfield combined to manage the Hollywood Canteen, the important center of entertainment on the West Coast for servicemen on leave, in which stars appeared as waiters, entertainers and even busboys.

Immediately after the outbreak of hostilities, the Office of War Information suggested to Warners that they, in common with other studios, concentrate on six categories: the Enemy, our Allies, the Armed Forces, the Production Front, the Home Front, and the Issues. As it happened, *Captains of the Clouds*, dealing with the Royal Canadian Air Force, *Across the Pacific*, which dealt with Japanese activities in the Pacific, *Wings for the Eagle*, which showed the efficiency of the Lockheed plant, and the patriotic musical, a biography of George M. Cohan, *Yankee Doodle Dandy*, had all been planned before Pearl Harbor. In the category the Enemy, *Edge of Darkness* was begun, together with a reworked version of *The Desert Song*, in which German activity in North Africa was shown. For the Armed Services, Warners prepared *Air Force*, based on the adventures of the crew of the Flying Fortress *Mary Ann;* for the Production Front, *Action in the North Atlantic*, about the merchant marine convoys to Murmansk; for the Home Front, *This Is the Army;* for the Issues, *Watch on the Rhine*, about a German refugee family, based on the play by Lillian Hellman.

The most important of the early war films, *Air Force* (1942) was made at the recommendation of General H. H. ("Hap") Arnold, commander of the U.S. Air Forces, a close friend of Jack Warner, who placed at the disposal of the director, Howard Hawks, Drew Field in Florida and several aircraft for the production.

Air Force, based on Dudley Nichols' screenplay, was the story of a B-17 (Flying Fortress) which took off from San Francisco for Hawaii just before Pearl Harbor and became involved in the Pacific conflict.

Captains Hewitt T. Wheless and Sam Triffy acted as technical advisers. Footage of the Battle of the Coral Sea was expertly fitted into the action by the editor, George Amy. The special effects camera work by Roy Davidson, Rex Wimpy and Fred Koenekamp was remarkable.

Despite the conventional portraits of the crew of the *Mary Ann*—from Captain Quincannon (John Ridgely) down to the bit players—the film was ideal propaganda material. It was stirring, exciting, evoking the feeling of being in action in the Pacific region. John Hughes' art direction kept skillfully to the confines of a B-17, and Franz Waxman's music had a patriotic glow.

Howard Hawks, who had had a great deal of flying experience, insisted upon detailed realism for the entire film. James Wong Howe, the cinematographer, had to solve a major problem in lighting the interior of the B-17 *Mary Ann* so that every detail could be made out on the screen. Since Hawks wanted a cabin roof constructed and made of a substance impenetrable to light, Howe had to use small lighting units called peanut globes, each the size of a thumbnail, hidden in and around the machinery so as to provide a polished gleam which illuminated tiny details. A major problem was to show the precise effect of a 350-mph gale lashing rain against the Plexiglas nose. Hawks personally instructed the special effects department in aiming air hoses against the necessary wind machines at precisely the correct velocity indicated.

One beautiful effect showed a flight of B-17s coming back to the airfield in the very late afternoon, with streaks of pale sunlight against a dove-gray sky. Just before the planes were due to come in, the generators failed, and Howe turned to Hawks saying, "What shall I do? We can't light the air strip." Hawks said, "That's not my problem." Howe obtained the aid of the special effects people, who came up with flares which extended all the way along the tarmac, and the effect of the flares, the streaks of shadow, and the smoke drifting across the jungle was very striking.

After its vigorous start, Warners did not proceed to

make films of importance concerning the Air Force during World War II. Instead, the emphasis moved to films romanticizing the deeds of the Navy, most notably Delmer Daves' *Destination Tokyo* (1943) written by Daves himself in collaboration with Albert Maltz, and *Action in the North Atlantic,* also made in 1943, written by John Howard Lawson, A. I. Bezzerides and W. R. Burnett and directed by Lloyd Bacon.

Destination Tokyo was the first film to illustrate the life on board a submarine in time of war; it benefited, in common with *Air Force,* from the complete cooperation of the appropriate authorities. The screenplay dealt with the journey of the U.S.S. *Copperfin* from San Francisco via the Aleutian Islands to a daring attack on the harbor of Tokyo, and the delivery of a sealed note which resulted in James A. Doolittle's famous raid. The sentimentality and heroics of the writing were tiresome, the direction assured. Lieutenant Commander Philip Compton and Chief Machinist's Mate Andy Lennox were given special leave from the Navy to act as technical advisers on the production, the latter a member of the crew of the submarine U.S.S. *Wahoo,* upon which the *Copperfin* was based. The skipper of the *Wahoo,* Lieutenant Commander Dudley Walker Morton, later worked closely with Delmer Daves, the special effects crew, and the cinematographer, Bert Glennon. The cast, led by Cary Grant playing a somewhat glamorous version of Morton, Alan Hale and John Ridgely travelled to Mare Island Navy Yard in San Francisco Bay, where they learned the elements of submarine life, and an understanding of the machinery to be reproduced in the artificial craft on the sound stage. Delmer Daves, a man with a knowledge of many sciences, personally supervised the construction of the *Copperfin,* working with a complicated map. *The New York Herald Tribune* reported: "Doors in the bulkheads that separate the watertight compartments are no more than oval openings, four

feet top to bottom and eighteen inches wide, the lower
edge a foot and a half from the floor deck. Acrobatics and
a good judgment of distance are required to negotiate
them."

The film was beautifully constructed, due to Daves'
extraordinary skill. The scene of the *Copperfin* entering
Yokohama Harbor became a classic of meticulously
directed suspense.

A companion piece to *Destination Tokyo,* made at the
behest of the Office of War Information in 1943, *Action in
the North Atlantic,* directed by Lloyd Bacon, was inspired by pictures and stories in *PM Magazine* about the
work of the merchant seamen. The intention of the script
was to quash complaints on the homefront about gasoline
rationing and the shortage of foodstuffs. It pointed out
that valuable supplies were being sent to the allies in
Russia.

Similar in construction to *Destination Tokyo,* the writing by John Howard Lawson, A. I. Bezzerides and W. R.
Burnett based on a story by Guy Gilpatric followed one
long voyage of a Liberty ship from the Atlantic via the
North Cape to the Arctic.

The set of the Liberty ship was among the most remarkable ever built in Hollywood. It filled one entire
stage. The funnels penetrated the rafters, and when the
huge 170-amp arc lights were installed to light it, they
looked to be merely the size of torch bulbs. Ted McCord,
the cinematographer, had a major problem of lighting the
set for day, twilight and night scenes, and of illuminating
the immense back projections of moving clouds and ocean
to suggest changes of weather and of light. The ship had
to give an impression of movement; it was too large to be
mounted on the hinged wooden rockers which had been
used for the galleons and privateer vessels in *The Sea
Hawk.* McCord and his operator were lifted by a massive
crane, which was so constructed that the camera could be

dipped, roll and rise again, giving the impression that the ship was pitching, yawing and rolling in a heavy swell. When there was a storm, thousands of gallons of water were thrown across the decks, hitting the players, and McCord had to solve the problem of supplying enough light for the cast to be seen through the sheets of rain and the leaping waves.

Another problem for McCord was showing the changing sunlight, which cast shadows of the ropes and rigging. The movement of the ship affected the movement of the shadows. McCord hung large arcs on the outside of the boat and moved them up and down so as to steer the correct intensity of light on his target.

The heat from the special effects flames and the powerful arc lights was so intense that at many points in the shooting Lloyd Bacon and his workmen had to wear smoke masks. *Life* magazine reported: "At one point director Bacon, who was in the wheelhouse of the tanker directing a close-up, ripped off his mask and was partly overcome by smoke. Twenty-five Burbank firemen were on the set at all times. Between takes, high-powered fans cleared away the dense smoke." At one stage, part of the studio roof was burned off. The result was a film of impressive realism, of action vividly sustained.

While these films dealt directly with the war in the air and on the sea, others dealt with espionage and spies with a sophisticated debunking humor. Among them was *All through the Night*, written by Leonard Spigeglass and Edwin Gilbert from a story by Spigelgass and Leonard Q. Ross. Influenced by *The Maltese Falcon*, made the year before, the picture combined elements of both the crime film and the anti-Nazi film, pitting Humphrey Bogart, as a virtual copy of the Dutch Schultz character played by Barton MacLane in *Bullets or Ballots*, against a Nazi *claque* headed by Peter Lorre and Conrad Veidt. The plot was among the most complicated on record, drawing from a number of early Warner situations in a vivid succession of chases, struggles, and hairsbreadth escapes; Frank McHugh, providing comic relief with examples of facetious humor as he had done for years, still further showed that the spy films of the time were descended from the crime movies of the early 1930s. Underlying the film was the cold ironical wit which by now had come to be a Warner trademark along with the snappy dialogue, the low-key photography, the violence and the smart direction of the players.

Following *All through the Night,* Warners made Raoul Walsh's *Background to Danger* (1942) with George Raft as an American secret agent, Sydney Greenstreet as a Nazi leader, and Peter Lorre as a Russian espionage specialist, in a story written by Eric Ambler and adapted by W. R. Burnett, about an attempt to defeat a possibility of Turkey entering the war with Germany. The material was absurd, and the direction, and Tony Gaudio's characteristic precision lighting were for once inadequate. More ambitious and elaborate, Curtiz' *Passage to Marseille* (1944), made the following year, had the advantage of drawing attention to the activities of the Free French. Humphrey Bogart, Sydney Greenstreet, Peter Lorre: the team was by now infallible, and the patriotism of the screenplay by Casey Robinson and Jack Moffitt, based on the novel by Charles Nordhoff and James Norman Hall, was quite convincing. The action began at the outset of the war in Europe, on board a French merchantman sailing out of Indo-China; upon leaving the Panama Canal, the ship collects a group of refugees from Devil's Island, all of whom are shown to be patriots. In a series of flashbacks, their true motives are disclosed.

Although the film was excessively long and the direction of Michael Curtiz too heavily Germanic, the production values were fine: James Wong Howe's photography, particularly in the Devil's Island sequences, had an in-

tricate beauty; and as always the art direction of Anton
Grot, moving effortlessly from a perfect reproduction of a
prison dormitory to that of an artificial jungle and a simple
farmhouse in France, was beyond praise.

A companion piece and successor, *Casablanca* (1942)
proved to be a greater triumph. The story department had
purchased an obscure play, *Everybody Goes to Rick's*,
which had not appeared on Broadway. It had been bought
because it was set in an exotic locale, Casablanca, dealt in
Nazi spies, and had as its focus a raffish cafe-bar, Rick's,
on which the writers could center a series of intrigues.
For the starring role of Ilsa—a girl married to a Resistance
leader, who falls in love with the café proprietor, Rick—
Jack Warner and Hal Wallis emphatically required Ingrid
Bergman, who was under contract to David O. Selznick.
At Jack Warner's suggestion, Wallis sent two distinguished scenarists, the twin brothers Julius and Philip
Epstein, to Selznick to tell him the story. Selznick agreed
to loan Miss Bergman. Meanwhile, Michael Curtiz was
assigned to the direction of the film.

When the Epsteins found some difficulty in transferring their ideas to the screen, Howard Koch was called in
for changes. After some weeks of discussions, the Epsteins finally withdrew, leaving Koch to give the material
some semblance of a story. When shooting began, Koch
had little more than a string of loosely connected episodes, enlivened largely by dialogue, transposed and oc-
casionally sharpened, which the Epsteins had be-
queathed him. Humphrey Bogart, impeccably cast as
Rick, the jaded but good-hearted male protagonist, helped
with some ideas. According to Koch, Curtiz promised to
direct the film with sufficient speed so that the many
holes in the plot, and the manifold absurdities of dialogue
and characterization, would go unheeded by the audience.

The resulting film was a success of technique over an

inordinately foolish, cliché-ridden, and quite obviously hastily written script. Each one of the characters was a stereotype, drawn from the pages of dime fiction: at the outset, Warner Brothers' familiar spinning globe, introduced in *Bullets or Ballots,* and used again in *Confessions of a Nazi Spy,* revolved as a Westbrook Van Voorhis-like voice attempted to give the proceedings an aura of *March of Time*-like verisimilitude. We are introduced to Rick's Cafe, a clip joint and gambling hall, the ersatz streets of Casablanca itself, and the Green Parrot Cafe presided over by the jovial Sydney Greenstreet. One by one we meet a collection of bizarre and nondescript characters: Captain Renault, owlish and immoral; Major Strasser, a Nazi gourmet, ordering caviar and murder in the same breath; Ugarte, a cowardly informer; Sam, a considerate black pianist. The vibrancy of the film consists not in these characters themselves, but in the acting, convincing and energetic, and in the Warner mood of patriotism, which sustained the action. The sequence in which the French people at Rick's stand to a defiant "Marseillaise" ideally evokes the feeling of a country at war.

Warners' next tribute to the Free French was *To Have and Have Not* (1944), a version of Hemingway's novel about a gun-runner in Florida, written by Jules Furthman and William Faulkner, directed by Howard Hawks, with Humphrey Bogart as the gun-runner Harry Morgan. The plot was changed to jell with the Warners' patriotic policy: instead of smuggling Chinese immigrants into the United States, Hemingway's hero played by Bogart smuggles Free French into Martinique under Vichy rule.

When the film was first announced, the Inter-American Affairs Committee under Nelson Rockefeller complained that it was unwise to set it in the original locale of Florida and Cuba, as it might unsettle the delicate relations with the Latin-American republics. As a result, Hawks pumped for Martinique.

In Havana in 1943, Howard Hawks, another cool and hard Warner director, had asked Hemingway, with whom he had been shooting dove and deep sea fishing off the coast of Cuba, whether he would like to write the script for the film. Hemingway was reluctant, feeling that he would be lost in the anonymity of the movie industry. Hawks told him, "It doesn't matter how you work. I can take your worst story and make a picture out of it." Hemingway asked: "What was my worst story?" And Hawks replied, "That piece of cheese called 'To Have and Have Not.'" Hemingway growled, "You can't make a picture out of that thing." Hawks suggested reducing the novel to the story of the leading protagonists. While the two men waited for the dove to come in or the fish to bite they talked the story out, but Hemingway still resolutely refused to come to Hollywood. Hawks bought the story for $80,000 and sold it to the studio at a considerable profit.

Hawks engaged his close friend William Faulkner to work on the script. Faulkner also liked to hunt and catch fish with Hawks, and they discussed many ideas on expeditions together. The bulk of the scenario suffered from expository rambling dialogue that would have worked in a novel but would not work on the screen, and a more experienced writer, Jules Furthman, was engaged to improve the writing and provide funny and idiomatic lines. But Faulkner was an excellent dramatist, enlivening every scene he touched.

For the heroine, a laconic and sultry girl whose insolent singing of erotic songs is the chief attraction of a Caribbean nightclub, Hawks cast Lauren Bacall. Hawks' wife had seen a picture of the girl in a New York magazine; when Hawks asked his secretary to contact Miss Bacall in New York, she accidentally sent the girl a train ticket. Miss Bacall arrived. She suffered from a high-pitched, unattractive voice. Hawks decided at once she was unsuitable. Within a week, she had taken voice lessons and acquired a pleasantly low-pitched, husky delivery he liked very much. He was intrigued by Miss Bacall's determined, cool, off-hand personality and impulsively granted her a screen test. She passed it with flying colors and Hawks immediately cast her opposite Humphrey Bogart in the picture.

Jules Furthman designed lines for her which were similar to those he had given Marlene Dietrich in scripts for films made by Josef Von Sternberg in the 1930s, basing her character on Miss Dietrich's, and even devising scenes in which, like the prototype, she leaned against doors and smoked, singing in a sexually provocative manner, or scored points off members of the cast in a coldly insulting fashion. The result was an entree to the American cinema as striking as Dietrich's in *Morocco*. Lauren Bacall's whisky-sour personality, as developed by Furthman and directed by Hawks, became as famous as Bogart's. Their mutual attraction, love affair and subsequent marriage not only gave the film its peculiar erotic tension, but made Bogart-Bacall a legend in the industry.

Hawks' direction was effective. He liked to place large groups of people in tiny, cramped rooms, with masses of shadows, which caused severe problems for his cinematographer, Sid Hickox. Hickox, in order to achieve sufficient light in these tiny sets had to hang incandescent 2000 watt lights just above the players' heads and about half an inch above the frameline, which caused intense heat. In some shots, 10,000 watt bulbs were used. The arc lights were placed on the floor, the cables so close to the actors' feet it was hard for them to avoid tripping. Certain lights were placed on the tops of the artificial walls: these caused an effect in which, if a player stood against the wall, there was a halo of backlight around his head and figure.

Because Hawks liked to have many shots below eye level, Hickox had a problem with his set ceilings: in wanting to hang the incandescent lights low, he had to remove most of the ceilings, but the camera shooting from the floor would reveal the lights themselves. So he set up ready-made three-quarter ceilings of butter muslin, just sufficiently dark to conceal the incandescents massed behind them, with the other incandescents only a fraction beyond the range of vision.

The film was characteristic of Warner pictures of the time: the ersatz exotic milieu, the largely nocturnal ambience, the cynical approach to sex, the stabs of violence, the bang 'em-up direction. It was a great success for the Warners, and received marevelous reviews.

In the spring of 1942, the War Office of Information was still urgently pressing for Warners' involvement with the propaganda machine. It urged Harry Warner to proceed with filming *Mission to Moscow*, the memoirs of Joseph E. Davies, former Ambassador to Russia. Despite the poor commercial results of *Confessions of a Nazi Spy*, Harry Warner acceded to this suggestion, which had been unsuccessfully put up to him and to Jack Warner by Jake Wilk of the story department in New York. At first, Davies had refused to consider the offers made to him, but he was impressed with Harry Warner and finally sent him a copy of the book with a personal note: "I'm sending my book over to you, and I wish you'd read it. If it's going to be made into a movie, I want you to make it. If you want to do it, write your own contract and I'll sign it." Davies supplied a great deal of material from his own diaries which had not been published in his book.

Davies personally approved Jack Warner's and Hal Wallis' choice of Walter Huston to play him in the picture. Interviewed by Ezra Goodman of *The New York Times* (March 7, 1943), Huston said: "My part in *Mission to Moscow* is really that of a sort of representative American—a kind of *Dodsworth* in a way. Although I'm playing the role of Joseph E. Davies, I don't resemble him a particle. I don't try to. The part is intended as a symbolic one—representing the American character and the typical American reaction to international events." Huston worked very closely with Davies on details of behavior and ambassadorial protocol, frequently engaging in lengthy conversations concerning the accuracy of his portrayal on the Bel Air golf course.

The making of the film was entrusted to the gifted producer Robert Buckner, and the screenplay was written by Howard Koch, who had illustrated his command of structure and of semi-documentary narrative in his famous script for Orson Welles' "War of the Worlds" broadcast. Carl Jules Weyl, working, like Koch, in close association with the historian Jay Leyda, rose to the task of re-creating Russia in the period of the outbreak of the war in Europe, while the research department prepared a selection of newsreel clips inserted effectively into the action. The film began with Davies discussing American isolationism and general disarmament with Schacht; observing the effect of Nazi training on children in Germany; mingling with the social set in Moscow; visiting steel mills and coal mines; attending the purge trials, a sequence which specifically accuses the Trotskyists of consorting with Germany and Japan in an attempt to overthrow the existing government; conferring with Stalin, who reveals that Chamberlain has allowed Germany's development in the hope that it would attack and defeat the Soviet Union; and pleading in vain for support from Russia in the United States just before Pearl Harbor.

Though Koch's script simplified and at times distorted the facts of that period of history, and though the portraits of Stalin by Mannart Kippen and of Churchill by the famous lawyer Dudley Field Malone were dinner party turns, the film was an impressive contribution to the war effort, attacking by implication those elements in American politics which had opposed the Warners' entry into propaganda before the commencement of the war. The physical execution was masterly: Michael Curtiz' direction had an epic grandeur, and the photography of Bert Glennon was extraordinary, particularly in the sequence of a rally in Madison Square Garden, in which Joseph E. Davies addresses an enormous crowd; and in the Presidium of the Military College in Moscow where the purge trials took place. Davies sat by the sound stage throughout a great deal of the shooting, marveling at the extraordinary accuracy of Weyl's sets. When a reporter, Ezra Goodman of the *New York Herald Tribune,* visited Davies, the trial sequence was being filmed. "This is . . . amazing," Davies said. "For a moment, it almost appeared as if I were back there, viewing the scene all over again." Not least of the film's manifold merits was Owen Marks' editing, which stitched together hundreds of disparate shots and evocation of a dozen countries into a fluid and exciting whole. Though the film's political content was negligible, not to say highly questionable, its propagandist verve was irresistible. It was a counterpart to the United States Army's celebrated "Why We Fight" series of documentaries, a parallel made forceful by the presence of Walter Huston, narrator of the army series.

After *Mission to Moscow* was released, a major controversy concerning the film's verisimilitude blew up in the pages of *The New York Times.* In May, 1943, the first bombshell burst, with a severe critique by the *Times* film reviewer, Bosley Crowther. Crowther, while applauding Warners for tackling once again a serious political theme, pointed out that in any such work the most absolute truth must be adhered to; any cheating with the facts, in works of pure propaganda, must be explained in an introductory note. And he made no bones about trouncing the studio for falsifying its portrait of Russia, showing a country bathed in benevolence, sunny extroversion, and good cheer. He also pointed out that the version of the Moscow trials of 1937 was very suspect indeed, too firmly opting for a theory that the Trotsky group had planned by means of a political coup to enable Germany to take over Russia. Crowther was particularly severe about the Davies family's introductory journey through the USSR: "[It shows them] on a Hollywood style tour . . . It shows them taking food at a railway station from a smiling peasant just like the old times. It shows that the Russian workers are just like the workers 'back home,'—that is, they work for wages and have a dutiful respect for the boss. It lets the American ladies know that their sisters in Russia get cosmetics from Mme. Molotoff's factory—only Mme. Molotoff is a svelte and suspiciously class-conscious dame. Her factory is decidedly Elizabeth Ardenish. And it makes a joke of the Ogpu." Crowther concluded: "Furthermore, the film is chronologically mixed up. It significantly makes it appear that Mr. Davies had a prescient conversation with Winston Churchill in 1939. Mr. Davies did report a conversation with Mr. Churchill—but in 1937, and it wasn't so apt. Such tricks have a way of imparting an omniscience to the Mr. Davies in the film, which is another form of distortion to aid the emotional impetus of the film.'

The same day in *The New York Times*, a letter appeared, co-signed by John Dewey, Professor of Philosophy at Columbia University, and Suzanne La Follette, secretary to her cousin, Robert M. La Follette, Sr. Dewey and Miss La Follette had been, respectively, chairman and secretary of the international commission of inquiry into the Moscow trials. Their letter, of great importance not only for its statement against the film, but because of the indication that intellectuals were now taking at least one studio's work very seriously indeed, is given in full:

The film "Mission to Moscow" is the first instance in our country of totalitarian propaganda for mass consumption—a propaganda which falsifies history through distortion, omission or pure invention of facts, and whose effect can only be to confuse the public in its thoughts and its loyalties.

Even in a fictional film this method would be disturbing. It becomes alarming in a film presented as factual and documentary and introducing living historical personalities. Our former Ambassador to the Soviet Union, Joseph E. Davies, personally introduces this dramatization of his mission as the "truth" about Russia. And the representation of President Roosevelt talking to Mr. Davies of the film seems to suggest that it is at least semi-official.

"Mission to Moscow" deals essentially with three things: Soviet history since January, 1937; international relations since that time, and American history since 1939. It falsifies all three.

The most important event in Soviet history during Mr. Davies' ambassadorship was Stalin's continuous purge. The film deals with only one aspect of it—the famous Moscow trials.

Immediately after Mr. Davies' arrival in Moscow— on Jan. 19, 1937—he is shown meeting, among others, at a diplomatic reception in his honor, Karl Radek, Nikolai Bukharin, and G. G. Yagoda.

Here the film borrows the primary technique of the Moscow trials in representing an event which could not have taken place. Karl Radek was arrested in September, 1936, and never released thereafter. The mass trial in which he was a principal began on Jan. 23, four days after the real Mr. Davies' arrival. Nikolai Bukharin was also under arrest at the time and was incriminated in Radek's "confession." Yagoda was already in disgrace. It is significant that in the book which the film purports to dramatize, Mr. Davies mentions none of these three men in listing his personal acquaintances among the accused.

The film telescopes the trial of 1937 and that of 1938. Dramatic license might possibly excuse representing Radek and Sokolnikov, principals in the 1937 trial, as principals with Bukharin, Krestinsky, and Yagoda in that of 1938, since all were allegedly in the same conspiracy and were actually tried. But there is no excuse for including as an accused in this synthetic trial Marshal Tukhachevsky, who was secretly executed in June, 1937, after no trial at all. To show Marshal Tukhachevsky, having his day in court may serve the interests of Soviet propaganda. It does not serve the interests of "truth about Russia."

In this synthetic trial the accused confess that their alleged crimes were directed by Trotsky. What is omitted is the testimony in the actual trials to specific alleged meetings with Trotsky abroad—testimony immediately challenged in the world press and conclusively disproved by evidence offered in rebuttal before the international commission of inquiry of which the undersigned were respectively chairman and secretary. It is not irrelevant to mention here that the commission, after painstaking investigation, concluded that the Moscow trials were frame-ups—a conclusion endorsed by intelligent world opinion at the time of its announcement.

The film falsifies not only the trials but Mr. Davies' own reports on them to the State Department and his comments in letters to individuals. On Page 52 of his book he says in a letter to Senator Byrnes: "The guarantees of the common law to protect the personal liberty of the individual from the possible oppressions of government . . . never impressed me with their beneficence in the public interest as they did in this trial. All of these defendants had been held incommunicado for months."

In the synthetic trial Mr. Davies' enthusiasm for the beneficent guarantes of the common law is not registered. What is registered is his close attention to the "confessions" (obligingly delivered in English, of course, since Mr. Davies knows no Russian) and his instant declaration of his conviction that the accused are guilty. There is no hint of the "reservation" recorded on Page 43 of his book, "based upon the facts that both the system of enforcement of penalties for the violation of law and the psychology of these people are so widely different from our own that perhaps the tests which I would apply would not be accurate if applied here."

In his official reports Mr. Davies said: "The terror here is a horrifying fact. There is a fear that reaches down into and haunts all sections of the community. No household, however humble, lives in constant fear of a nocturnal raid by the secret police. Once the person is taken away, nothing of him or her is known for months—and many times never—thereafter." (Page 302).

But the make-believe Russia of the film is gay, even festive, and wherever Mr. Davies goes he encounters a happy confidence in the regime.

In his letters and reports Mr. Davies spoke of the terror as a struggle for power—"This particular purge is undoubtedly political." (Page 303); "The Stalin regime, politically and internally, is probably stronger than heretofore. All potential opposition has been killed off." (Page 202).

The film, on the other hand, gives the impression that Stalin is killing off not potential political opponents but traitors in the service of foreign powers. In other words, it reflects the sudden belated flash of illumination described by Mr. Davies in the section of the book called "A Study in Hindsight," which revealed to him (in Wisconsin, and not until June, 1941) that the terror was really a purge of fifth columnists.

The film represents Stalin as having been driven into Hitler's arms by the Franco-British policy of appeasement. There is no reference to the desperate efforts of France and Britain to reach a defensive alliance with Stalin in 1939, no reference to the presence in Moscow of an Allied military mission vainly waiting to confer with the Soviet General Staff at the very time when the Stalin-Hitler pact was announced. Hitler's armies are shown invading Poland, but not Stalin's.

There is no mention of the Soviet Government's demand for a negotiated peace after Stalin and Hitler had divided Poland, or of Stalin's words after the partition, "Our friendship is cemented with blood," or of Molotov's famous remark that "fascism is just a matter of taste," or of Mr. Davies' own reference to "Russian ally, Germany." (Mission to Moscow, Page 474.)

Nor is there in the film even the merest hint that in France, England, the United States—wherever the Communist International was functioning—the Communist parties systematically sabotaged the Allied cause. One would never know that the most determined and noisy isolationists in this country before June 22, 1941, were in the Communist-led American Peace Mobilization. One would never know that for months before that date the Communists fomented strikes in our defense industries, calculated to sabotage our rearmament and our aid to Britain. Communist responsibility for these strikes is a matter of record—read the statements at the time of Attorney General Jackson, high-ranking labor leaders and the entire American press.

The film is subtly anti-British. It harps on the appeasement policy of Chamberlain and represents Mr. Churchill only in the period when he was still in the opposition and comparatively powerless. By the device of leaping over Stalin's collaboration with Hitler and Churchill's direction of British affairs, it conveys the impression that Stalin's foreign policy has always been democratic and anti-fascist and Britain's one of appeasement. One would never suspect that it was Stalin who enabled Hitler to attack Poland and Chamberlain who came to Poland's defense.

The whole atmosphere of the film conveys the impression that Soviet Russia is our ally in the same degree as Great Britain. The Japanese Ambassador is snubbed and insulted at the same diplomatic reception where Mr. Davies could not have met Bukharin and Radek. Mr. Davies is shown visiting a hospital where Russian doctors and nurses are tending Chinese victims of Japanese air raids—though how they got to Moscow is not explained. The doctor in charge tells him that "the Chinese are our friends," and points the moral of the dire results of appeasement.

The effect of all this is to create the impression that the Soviet Union is our ally against Japan. In fact Japan and Soviet Russia have a non-aggression pact to this day; and it must be said for Mr. Stalin that he has never sought to mislead the United States about his policy of neutrality in the Far Eastern war. Nothing could be more dangerous than to mislead the American people into believing that the Soviet Union will turn against Japan the moment Hitler is defeated.

The film shows Mr. Davies, back in America, making a swing around the circle in spite of ill health, because it is his "duty" to explain Russia to the American people. The drama of this section is achieved through contrasting flashes—a wild anti-conscription meeting followed by a flash of Mr. Davies explaining Russia; meetings of American business men demanding isolation and business with Hitler, followed by flashes of Mr. Davies explaining Russia. And so on.

Now what are the facts? On July 15, 1941, Mr. Davies told Sumner Welles that he wished to be of every possible help to the Soviet Embassy here ("Mission to Moscow," Page 492). His swing around the circle took place in the Winter of 1941 and 1942—mostly in 1942. The Conscription Act was passed by Congress in September, 1940; and one of the dissenting votes was cast by Representative Vito Marcantonio.

Obviously Mr. Davies' swing around the circle had nothing to do with swinging American opinion behind conscription. Neither had it anything to do with dis-

suading such American business men as may have
wanted to do business with Hitler, for Pearl Harbor
was bombed on Dec. 7, 1941, and American business
men were just as much against Hitler as was Mr. Davies. Mr. Davies' swing around the circle was no battle
royal. It was just an unexciting trip to sell the Soviet
Government to an American public already 100 per
cent for the Russian people in their magnificent defense of their country.

Finally, a sinister totalitarian critique of the parlia-
mentary system is introduced in the film. The traditional isolationism of some American members of
Congress before the war is represented as equivalent
to pro-nazism. The whole effort is to discredit the
American Congress and at the same time to represent
the Soviet dictatorship as an advanced democracy.
Such gross misrepresentation can only contribute to
confusion in our relations with the Soviet Union. If
our collaboration is to continue after the war it cannot
be on the basis of Soviet propaganda but only on that
of genuine understanding of the differences in our political systems.

The film is, to resume, anti-British, anti-Congress,
anti-democratic and anti-truth. It deepens that crisis in
morals which is the fundamental issue in the modern
world. The picture "Mission to Moscow" and similar
propaganda have helped to create a certain moral cal-
lousness in our public mind which is profoundly un-
American. Only recently the American people received with comparative calm the Soviet Government's announcement that it had executed as "Nazi
agents" the two Polish Jews, Ehrlich and Alter, inter-
nationally known leaders of Socialist labor whom it
had arrested when it invaded Poland. A few more un-
critically accepted films like "Mission to Moscow"—
for where thousands read books, millions see motion
pictures—and Americans will be deadened to all
moral values.

"Mission to Moscow" is a major defeat for the democratic cause. In putting out this picture the producers, far from rendering the patriotic service on which Mr. Davies compliments them, have assailed the very foundations of freedom. For truth and freedom are indivisible, as Hitler knew when he expounded his method of confusing public opinion through propaganda. The picture "Mission to Moscow" makes skillful use of the Hitler technique. To quote Matthew Low of the New Leader: "This kind of 'truth' is on the march, and God help us if nothing can stop it."

Many further letters in this vein arrived at the office of the *Times*. They were replied to at length by Howard Koch in the issue of June 13, 1943:

When a picture has caused as much controversy as "Mission to Moscow" and is described both as "the most memorable document of our time" and "propaganda which falsifies history," it seems to me that such divergent opinions from equally responsible citizens must reflect conflicting attitudes in the political subject-matter more than on the picture itself. However, in his temperate analysis of the film in a recent Sunday column, *The Times'* critic suggests that those entrusted with writing and producing pictures have a grave responsibility when they deal factually with contemporary themes of vital importance to human beings everywhere in the world—and this is undoubtedly true. As author of the screenplay, I feel it may be illuminating to the public, and even to the film's detractors, to make a clear statement of how we endeavored to discharge that responsibility.

First of all, what was our intention—to "whitewash" Russia, as some critics glibly sum it up? No, "Whitewash" implies painting white over a darker color, thus assuming that we had unfavorable preconceptions about the Soviet Union which we were anxious to cover up.

Frankly, I was as confused as most other people on

the actual role the Soviet Union was playing in the tur-
moil of world events, and Mr. Davies' brilliant, legalis-
tic fact-finding and reporting gave me the first impression of an objective appraisal that I could trust.
However, the canvas of our picture soon expanded
beyond the boundaries of the book, and many other
valid sources of information had to be tapped in an attempt to fit each actor into his true historic role.

Next came the molding of these events into a dramatic pattern—and in this process factual liberties had
to be taken. How else could a coherent story be told in
two hours? History provides us with the materials of
drama, but it doesn't conveniently arrange them into
scenes or bind them to any unifying theme. That is the
province of the dramatist as distinct from the historian.

But here it must be admitted that the decisions
were not easy. When is the changing of a fact the
perversion of a truth? As nearly as I can state it, we
regarded a fact inviolable as long as that fact represented an underlying truth which was significant to
the audience's understanding and evaluation of the
conduct of a nation or of an individual in the unfolding
political events.

Let us consider an example: The most prevalent
objection on the part of the picture's critics seems to
be the telescoping of the two "purge" trials into one.
Thus defendants who never actually appeared
together are tried in the same court room in the film.
This seemed to us justifiable, since months of testimony had to be concentrated into minutes of time, and
since the consequent liberties with fact did not alter
the substance of what the defendants confessed—
taken from an authenticated transcript of the trial.

Another important accusation against the film's authenticity is the statement that it loads the political
dice on the side of the Soviet leaders and against the
English and French appeasers. Here I can only refer
the objectors to the records as I found them—Soviet
defense of the League and collective security at Ge-

neva (minutes of the League Assembly); Soviet aid to the legal people's government of Spain invaded by fascist armies (newspaper records); Soviet readiness to give military support to Czechoslovakia if the French Government kept its treaty obligation to come to that country's aid against Germany (direct unequivocal statement made during the crisis by the Soviet Government and confirmed by President Benes), and finally, the repeated but unheeded pleas of Stalin and other Soviet leaders for an ironclad military alliance of the democratic powers.

And equally clear are the records of the English and French Governments during that critical period in facing the same questions. The history of appeasement from the breakdown of the League to the last minute, when they knew war with Germany was inevitable despite all their concessions, is not a pretty record —and apparently it's not what our critics would like to expose to the public.

If, in the film, the President of the United States seems "omniscient"—as some of our critics complain—and his reactionary and isolationist opponents seem incredibly blind or even sinister, we did not invent the contrast. Again I refer the objectors to the records—even the Congressional records.

It is also contended that we give Russia's side of the Finnish dispute without giving Finland's. Judging by the gasp that goes up from the audience when Davies gives a clear statement of why the Russians went into Finland, it seems evident that Finland's side, and only Finland's, was very well publicized.

Finally, many fingers are pointed at us for not showing the less favorable internal aspect of the Soviet experiment. To a certain extent this is a valid criticism. In dramatizing Ambassador Davies' entry into Russia we made the mistake of portraying him and his family too quickly convinced of the well-being of the Soviet people and the benevolence of their government. However, in fairness let me point out that Mr.

Davies does find imperfections and shortcomings in Soviet achievements during the course of the picture.

In pursuing our purpose of projecting the simplified but essential historical truth of this period, certain "heroes" emerged—the President of the United States, the statesmen of the Soviet Union, the present Prime Minister of Great Britain and other men of good-will who foresaw what was happening and did all in their power to avert the tragedy of war. Now some people obviously don't like the "heroes"—they find them politically distasteful. These elements have a right to their preferences. Their quarrel is, however, not with us or the picture of Mr. Davies but with history itself—history which in recent years has been unkind to their prejudices.

Despite the sturdiness of this letter, there can be no doubt that *Mission to Moscow* severely injured Warners' prestige, and that political critics damaged its popular reception. After World War II, as a later chapter will show, the film became, in fact, an embarrassment, mentioned as it was in the House Un-American Activities Committee's investigations of Hollywood, and forcing Jack Warner into the unhappy position of wishing he had never made that lavish and controversial, superbly made but ill-written picture in the first place.

12

On
the Home Front

Whileを WARNERS CELE-
brated the activities of the Air Force, the merchant marine, the men of the submarines, the Free French and
the Russians, Jack Warner, Hal Wallis and Steve Trilling
also recognized the necessity for providing films which
would act as opiates for the women at home. Deprived of
their husbands, brothers and sons, millions of American
women patronized the movies with an intensity that was
unprecedented even during the earliest years of the talkies. In supplying them with escapist fantasies, or stories
of female suffering so intense that they could forget their
own misery by living vicariously through the heroine on
the screen, the studio obtained the most substantial box
office returns in its history. Entering a theatre, munching

tubs of popcorn, women felt an intoxication, a sense of being hypnotized, as the Warner shield appeared on the screen, the titles dissolved in an hallucinatory light, and Bette Davis, Joan Crawford or Ann Sheridan emerged from the flattering Gaudio, Polito or Haller shadows to do battle with the world. The care devoted to these films was as great as that devoted to the more important films of the previous decade, the narcotic pulsing music of Steiner, Korngold and Franz Waxman, cheerfully plagiarizing Tchaikovsky, Brahms and Wagner (Steiner's score for *The Gay Sisters* consisted of variations on the "Siegfried Idyll," rewritten for full orchestra) in order to suffuse the senses. It was usual for each heroine to be given her own lilting or tripping theme on the solo violin, augmented by trumpet if she became angry and violent, while the villain was often symbolized by a deep bass sound of the full orchestra, achieved partly by "milking" the microphone.

The matrix of the women's pictures of the war years had been prepared pre-war—in 1940: Edmond Goulding's film *The Great Lie* turned out to be the foundation of the structure of fantasy which became desirable to women in the period. It was of the essence of the mode that women should be the chief protagonists of the drama, that they should live in conditions of extreme luxury, and that they should be dressed as glamorously as possible by the Warner designer, Orry-Kelly. In order to increase the sense of wish-fulfilment, the heroines were frequently gifted in one field of art or another: Bette Davis, in her films of the period, was a mistress of embroidery (*The Letter*), wood carving (*Now, Voyager*), pianism (*Deception*), poetry (*Winter Meeting*) and fiction (*Old Acquaintance*). In *The Great Lie* Miss Davis owned a mansion the size of the White House only a short distance from Washington, D.C. (in Maryland), a private landing field, a husband (played by George Brent) who resembled Jack Warner and, in common with Warner, was something important in the Air Force,* and a fine range of clothes. Her income was so large that she could supply a trust fund to the pianist in return for obtaining the custody of her baby.

The plot, contrived by Lenore Coffee from a novel by Polan Banks entitled *Far Horizon*, must be recorded in full, because it was the quintessence of Forties fantasy, the antithesis of the realistic stories which had made Warners famous only a few years before.

First of all, the credits: following the Warner shield and the customary fanfare, a woman's hands are seen playing over a set of piano keys, while the titles are scrawled across the image in a feminine copperplate. A maid tries to straighten an apartment after a party given by the pianist Sandra Kovak (Mary Astor); in a mansion in Maryland, her rival, Maggie (Bette Davis) waits for the homecoming of Pete (George Brent) by private plane from Washington, D.C. Pete is about to leave on a secret mission. He has married Sandra on an impulse, but their marriage has been proven illegal by virtue of her previous betrothal. Now he marries Maggie. But Sandra is carrying his child. Pete is reported missing while flying over Brazil. Maggie offers Sandra financial security in return for the baby. After an impatient Sandra, watched over by Maggie, has the baby in secrecy in Arizona, Pete unexpectedly turns up. Now Sandra wants to renege on her bargain. But seeing how happy Maggie is with Pete, she changes her mind and decides to devote her future to the piano.

Nobody at the time, excepting the critics and the two female stars, who constantly rewrote the script during the production, questioned the veracity of these events. An earlier film, *The Letter* (1940) directed by William Wyler and written by Howard Koch—based on Somerset Maugham's short story and play about a murderous

---

* Jack Warner was commissioned Lieutenant Colonel in 1942.

woman in Malaya—had already proven that Bette Davis, faced with a tense emotional situation, was cast-iron "box office." When war broke out, she continued in a cycle of romantic fantasies, trying, usually without success, to give them some semblance of realism by insisting upon changes in the writing. Her first film of the war was *Now, Voyager* (1942), directed by Irving Rapper from a script by Casey Robinson based on a novel by Olive Higgins Prouty. Here again the wish-fulfilment fantasy, realized with great skill by director, writer and star, is 27-carat soap. Charlotte, played by Miss Davis, is an ugly, bespectacled girl living with a repressive mother in a mansion in Boston. She has a nervous breakdown; she is taken in hand by Dr. Jaquith, a psychiatrist whose expensive sanitarium, Cascade, provides a partial cure. She emerges as a fashion plate. Her physician recommends a luxury pleasure cruise to the Caribbean and South America. On board the ship she meets Jerry, a Continental architect escaping an unhappy marriage. He puts two cigarettes in his mouth at one time, lights them, and hands her one. While touring Rio, their taxi crashes and they "bundle" for the night. The result is that Charlotte understands herself as a woman. She agrees to become a Back Street mistress, secretly becoming a second mother to Jerry's ugly daughter Tina, whom she and Dr. Jaquith cure of her inferiority complex. In the last scene, Charlotte says to Jerry while the camera dollies out of the window to a backdrop of the sky, "Why ask for the moon? We have the stars."

The film was an enormous success. In *Old Acquaintance* (1943) directed by Vincent Sherman, the star was a novelist in conflict with another writer, played by Miriam Hopkins, and contributing to the war effort by making a radio speech; the action somewhat monotonously resolved itself into a series of squabbles between the two women in surroundings of opulent oppressiveness. In Sherman's *Mr. Skeffington*, made in 1944, based on the novel by "Elizabeth," Miss Davis played a flighty society woman who is made to become decent and honest by losing her hair in an attack of diphtheria. When her husband, blinded in World War II, still sees her as a beauty, she is humbled before him.

It would be futile to dwell on the "qualities" of these films. They were, like the stories which filled *Redbook* or the *Ladies' Home Journal*, necessary bromides, served to the suffering in time of war. They ensured "a good cry," and they helped earn the studio many millions of dollars worth of wartime profits by the year 1944.

Another genre which appealed strongly to women was that of the "literary biography," the "prestige picture," or versions of the lush novels which were constantly bought and read to while away lonely evenings with the menfolk away.

Here again the quality was well below the standard Warners had set in the 1930s. Although executed with skill by the director, Irving Rapper, and photographed by Polito, a sure mark of quality, *The Adventures of Mark Twain* (1944) was a pedestrian and loosely constructed account of the life of the novelist; and *Devotion* (1946), a life of the Brontës, was a wholly ill-advised travesty of the facts. More satisfactory, though scarcely more convincing, three biographies of light-music composers were made with the entire studio's resources, and were decent examples of Warner craftsmanship: *Yankee Doodle Dandy* (George M. Cohan, 1942), *Rhapsody in Blue* (George Gershwin, 1945), and, made just after the war, *Night and Day* (Cole Porter, 1946).

During the war, the studio had purred along quite smoothly despite the draining off of more than 300 employees, and Jack Warner's frequent absences as a Lieutenant Colonel in the United States Air Force working for

"Hap" Arnold on specific secret projects. The only severe blow had been the bombing of the Warner Brothers studio in Great Britain, with the loss of the manager and other members of the personnel. Harry and Albert Warner worked comfortably on both coasts.* The last year of the war was the studio's most successful to date, with over 10 million dollars in net profits.

It was in 1945 with the onset of peace that a whole series of urgent problems disrupted the calmness of the studio operation. Almost immediately, the mood of the country changed, and with it the mood of many of Warners' contracted employees. When the wage and price scale was unfrozen, following a wartime ordinance, many employees became restless, feeling they were inadequately paid. Hal Wallis left the studio with his associate, Joseph Hazen, when Jack Warner attempted to accept an Oscar given to Wallis at an Academy Award celebration. Following this turn of events, Jack Warner took over as head of production himself, with Steve Trilling as his second-in-command. There was a great deal of tension between the two men. In January, 1946, a major collision with a star occurred, similar to that involving Bette Davis in the 1930s. Joan Leslie, a pretty but inadequate actress who had been given several major roles beyond her capacity, had somewhat ungratefully grown impatient with the studio which fostered her career. She had been signed at the age of 17, her contract, approved by the Superior Court, carrying the usual six month option clauses with a continually rising salary when the options were renewed. She was working in a comedy entitled *Two Guys from Milwaukee* when she became 21, on January 26, 1946. She finished the film, and then notified Warners that she wished to disaffirm her minority contract.

Warners firmly exercised its next option for Miss Les-

---

* David Warner had died of encephalitis in 1939.

lie's services and suspended her. She announced that she would at once work for United Artists as the star of a production by Seymour Nebenzahl, *The Chase*. Her lawyer argued that this was improper, and Judge Paonessa of the Superior Court in Los Angeles voided the injunction, saying that Miss Leslie's contract was invalid, due to her minority at the time it was signed. Obstinately, Warners' legal department fought a losing battle all the way up to December 13, 1948, when Miss Leslie was released from her contract. She went on to a steadily declining career.

In the summer of 1945, labor problems came to a head in Hollywood. The Conference of Studio Unions went on strike the following day, claiming that studios had failed to meet a demand for a 36-hour weekly guarantee and better working conditions. A major dispute was between the painters' union and the IATSE over the question of set decorators, who, the painters' union claimed were interfering with their right to paint flats. In August, picketers attacked people entering the Warner Brothers Theatre on Hollywood Boulevard. In October, full-scale riots broke out. The focus of these disturbances was at Warners. One Thursday night, Herbert Sorrell, president of the Conference of Studio Unions, held a secret meeting at Hollywood Legion Stadium. An angry worker suggested placing 100 picketers outside Warners to prevent all production staff from entering the studio. The picket line began at 5 AM. By 7 AM it had increased to almost one thousand. When a studio policeman tried to drive in, the picketers stormed his car and tipped it over. Burbank police managed to set up a no-man's-land, with the picketers and non-picketing members of the IATSE divided up. As more workers arrived, fierce fights broke out. One man, Chester L. Estep, was slugged by a socket wrench. An ex-marine, Paul A. Wells, was beaten unconscious when he tried to cross the picket line. A gas bomb went off, injuring the eye of Helen McCall, a secretary. A painter, A. Rieser, was stabbed in the nose and forehead.

By noon, Chief of Police Horrall of Los Angeles and Chief of Police Verne Rasmussen of Glendale had brought in more than 200 men with steel helmets, gas masks and clubs. At twelve o'clock, Blayney Mathews, former chief investigator for the District Attorney's office and for many years chief of the studio police, thrust through the picketers. Bleeding and bruised, he ordered the studio firemen to turn their hoses on the mob. The pickets fought back with a barrage of bottles, brickbats and stones. The studio piled tables upon tables to set up a barricade, while the picketers made a defense line of cars.

By one o'clock, Horrall finally lost his patience. With tear gas and clubs, his men stormed in and struck down everyone who stood in their way. When the crowd was finally cleared, Sorrell and eight aides were arrested on a charge of contravening the riot act.

On October 7, 600 picketers crowded into Warners' Olive Street entrance, despite a Superior Court ruling which restricted all access to entrances to eighteen people. On October 8, at the Hollywood Legion Stadium, a mass meeting was held, addressed by the writer Dalton Trumbo, protesting against police methods at the time of the strike. On October 9, another battle broke out at Warners. This time, eight people were arrested and 70 wounded, in an almost exact repetition of the events of three days earlier. Hundreds of non-striking employees set up beds in their offices, from simple prop room mattresses to art department beds slept in by Bette Davis in *Jezebel* and *Queen Elizabeth*, or by George Arliss in *Disraeli*.

The riots continued for days. One man, a former comedian named Porky Hall, the fat boy in the "Our Gang" comedies, was severely injured by the enraged crowd when he attempted a charge through the ranks. On October 11, 400 picketers were arrested on charges of rioting and failure to disperse, singing "The Star Spangled Banner" as police moved in with guns. There seemed to be some evidence that Communists had inspired the strike. *The Los Angeles Times* in an editorial dated October 12, 1945, said: "The Communists are trying to take over the studios to make use of films for their own propaganda."

The strike finally ended on October 25, following a meeting in Cincinnati between William Green, president of AFL, and Eric Johnston, head of the Motion Picture Producers' Association. In 1946, the strike problem emerged again. Members of the CSU refused to work on sets built by IATSE members which became known as "hot seats." On September 28, the entire episode of the fall of 1945 was repeated almost identically, with fights between picketers and police at both Warners and MGM. It was weeks before new negotiations once more settled the matter.

As a direct result of the strike, widespread feeling began in Hollywood that a Communist plot was being hatched to disrupt production. Naturally, this feeling was particularly strong at Warners, the focus of the strike. When the House Un-American Activities Committee under J. Parnell Thomas began its first inquiries into Communism in Hollywood in January, 1947, it found a ready ear in Jack Warner and his associates. Already, a number of writers whom Warner claimed to have found guilty of sneaking Communist ideas into their scripts had been let go, among them John Howard Lawson and Albert Maltz.

In October, 1947, in the Caucus Chambers of the Old House Office Building in Washington, the first major hearings of the Committee resulted in the imprisonment of the "Hollywood Ten," writers including Lawson and Maltz who had taken the First Amendment, refusing to say whether they were or were not Communists. They were charged with acting in contempt of Congress. Jack

Warner appeared at the hearings, asserting that he had long been aware of Communist attempts to insert left-wing arguments into Warner scripts: he specifically named Clifford Odets, Alvah Bessie, Ring Lardner, Jr., Albert Maltz and John Howard Lawson. Needless to say, he was questioned closely about *Mission to Moscow:* he disclosed that it had been, as many people had suspected from the first despite disclaimers by both Joseph E. Davies and Howard Koch, made specifically on Roosevelt's advice.

Aside from the harassments of the "Communist threat," and the spectacular rise of television, the Warners were plagued by another major problem in those immediate post-war years. For a decade, successive Attorneys General had sought to break the monopolistic hold of the studios on theatre chains throughout the country, chains which insured and guaranteed the release of a motion picture. Jack and Harry Warner had fought these campaigns against the studios, insisting that the whole basis of the film industry lay in having its own immediate outlets for its products. But on July 26, 1949, Warners, together with Loew's and Fox, was ordered to divorce its theatre holding interests from producing and distributing units, and many theatres had to be sold.

By the end of the war, it appeared that a change had taken place in the caliber of Warner productions. Whereas in the 1930s, the technical approach had sometimes been too rushed and rough-and-ready, and the writing by contrast had been almost consistently brilliant in its acid realism, in the 1940s the reverse was true. The war propaganda films, with their false heroics, grossly distorted sentimentalized cracker-barrel portraits of soldiers, airmen and navy personnel, had nevertheless been banged across with all of the immense skill the studio could command. The women's pictures and popular biographies combined *schmaltz* with adeptness in presentation. It was not until late 1945 that the position improved, and that the writing again began to assume the intensity of the best work of the 1930s.

13

Post-War
Pessimism

THE MAN RESPONSIBLE FOR
the new wave of *films noirs* was the producer Jerry Wald,
whose works of the early 1940s, *Man Power*, with Marlene Dietrich and Edward G. Robinson, and *They Drive
by Night*, with George Raft and Ida Lupino, had been
dark portraits of the lives of power linesmen and truckers.
In the direct line of Warners policy, Wald believed in
making films with which ordinary people could identify,
but he added a touch of bitterness and hard pessimism to
the mixture which made the films very much his own.

Jerry Wald had worked on magazines and as a radio
writer before breaking into Warners in the 1930s. He was
supposed to have been the basis for Budd Schulberg's
hustling Sammy Glick in *What Makes Sammy Run*. He
was a compulsive worker who hated to rest. Mild in ap-

pearance, pallid with slightly protuberant, earnest eyes, he was in fact a dynamo. He cast ideas—few of them new—around to everyone. He had a mind like a cuckoo's nest. He assembled facts and stories. He reworked past stories, convincing only himself that what he did was original.

Wald particularly liked the bitter urban novels of James M. Cain, whose *Double Indemnity,* filmed at Paramount by Billy Wilder in 1943, had sparked off a cycle of similar works at the tail end of the war, beginning with Cain's own *The Postman Always Rings Twice.* Wald wanted to follow these with a version of Cain's *Mildred Pierce,* the story of a frustrated suburban housewife in Glendale, California, seized with ambition for her daughter. Into the book, Cain had poured all that he knew—and that was a great deal—about the materialist ambitions of ordinary Americans. The book was full of observations of sexual and financial deals, written in a hard-bitten style.

The first script was written by Catherine Turney, who had just adapted a version of Somerset Maugham's *Of Human Bondage.* When Wald wanted her to prepare rewrites, she had already been engaged by Curtis Bernhardt and Bette Davis to work on Miss Davis' independent picture *A Stolen Life.* Wald decided to reconstruct her material within flashbacks, the story told by various witnesses in a police station. The technique sprang not from the novel, but in part from Orson Welles' *Citizen Kane,* in part from Jerry Wald's close viewings of *Double Indemnity,* which also had a flashback structure. Wald's chief difference with Miss Turney lay in his concern with the character of Mildred's daughter Vida, a spoiled girl whose ambitions led her to commit murder. In the novel, and in Miss Turney's screenplay, Vida rose to some professional success, trained in Pasadena as a musician. Jerry Wald insisted that left to her devices she would sink into a sleazy, defiant role as a nightclub singer. It was a very

"Warners" concept and it worked, despite Cain's violent objections in a series of letters.

Allowing for certain minor compromises, the film showed a renewed maturity on the part of the studio, harking back to the realism of the 1930s. The script, rewritten by Ranald MacDougall, was admirably frank; it defied the Hays office in its treatment of sex and money, disclosing with heartless brilliance the precise quality of California.

In other hands the story might have been rendered maudlin, but Cain's constant precision of detail was adhered to painstakingly. Mildred Pierce (Joan Crawford) buys a second husband in marriage. Her daughter is shown as worthless, a vicious product of over-indulgence. None of the characters, with the possible exception of the female protagonist, is spared. The squalid salesman Wally Fay (Jack Carson), the weak first husband (Bruce Bennett), the mannish secretary of the Pierce empire (Eve Arden), the failed millionaire-turned-gigolo (Zachary Scott): played with a savage edge, these are all shrewdly observed portraits, realizing perfectly Cain's concept. The physical execution shows Curtiz at his best, and Ernest Haller's photography has a quintessential Warner look. Joan Crawford's performance, her finest on the screen, won an Oscar. Anton Grot, who designed several sequences, sketch by detailed sketch, provided credit titles which had a baroque flourish: printed on rocks, they were washed off by the Pacific waves one by one.

Inevitably, Jerry Wald thrust Joan Crawford into a new series of *films noirs*, beginning with *Humoresque* (1946), a very well-made but foolish story of a rich woman and a musician, directed by the skillful Jean Negulesco, and *Possessed* (1947) directed by Curtis Bernhardt, based by Ranald MacDougall and Sylvia Richards on the magazine story by Rita Weiman, in which the star played a woman driven into a psychotic breakdown. Once again, the *mi-*

lieu of Los Angeles was effectively realized. The opening was shot in the downtown section of Los Angeles, the unhappy woman played by Miss Crawford wandering through the bleak streets at dawn, a streetcar clanging loudly past her, filled with depressed and gray-faced citizens. Joseph Valentine's photography, hard and stark and clear, and Anton Grot's designs, particularly of the hospital scenes, brilliantly created a world sterilized and devoid of hope.

Curtiz' *Flamingo Road* (1947) again combining Wald, Curtiz and Crawford, was less convincing, though the portrait given in Robert Wilder's script, from his own novel, of life in a Southern town was no less rancid than Ranald MacDougall's portraits of California. Superior in every way, *The Damned Don't Cry* (1950) directed by Vincent Sherman, gave a convincing account of Mafia activities in Los Angeles and Palm Springs. Produced by Jerry Wald, the film was an uncompromising portrait of greed. The author of the original story, Gertrude Walker, actually spent some time living with gangsters in the California desert. The "taste" of the underworld was perfectly hit off: the film had an emanation of evil. In one cold, relentless sequence, as the ambitious girl played by Crawford learned her instructions from Selena Royle in the art of behaving as a society woman among the leading members of the gang, the film achieved an extraordinary level of intensity.

A companion piece to the Joan Crawford vehicles was Vincent Sherman's *Nora Prentiss* (1946), adapted by N. Richard Nash from an original story by Paul Webster and Jack Sobell, photographed by James Wong Howe in a series of flowing dark images, low-key and *blafard*, designed by Anton Grot in a perfect evocation of San Francisco. The story of a doctor, too weak to break with his wife, involved with a singer, could on the face of it be taken as a melodramatic contrivance. But the portrait of character is completely unsparing: the dull husband, played with sympathetic understanding by Kent Smith, the seedy down-at-heel singer, tenderly realized by Ann Sheridan, the wife who is her own worst enemy (Rosemary DeCamp). The treatment is of a Gallic order of realism. As in so many of the Warner pictures of the period, we move like dream-walkers through a world of night: of wet streets, cramped hotel rooms, a shabby nightclub, a road crowded with traffic, a car suddenly bursting into sheets of flame.

In oddly corrupted forms, the Warner musical, the gangster and the action film movie re-emerged as quintessential *films noirs* of the late 1940s and early 1950s. In the first category, Curtiz' *Young Man with a Horn* adapted by Carl Foreman and Edmund G. North from the novel by Dorothy Baker, was a stark portrait of a jazz trumpeter, Rick Martin, based indirectly on the career of Bix Beiderbecke. The script treated Martin's emergence from a sensitive and lonely boyhood to a neurotic, overwrought adult, played with dynamic attack by the young Kirk Douglas. His only warmth is shown in his friendship with Art Hazzard (Juano Hernandez), his black friend and mentor: in its portrayal of Hazzard, shown here as sensitive, considerate and gifted, the film was ahead of its time. Yet the overall impression is one of pessimism, a flavor of coldness drawn from the novel itself.

Ted McCord's photography was a marvelous support for Curtiz' energetic, forceful direction. McCord's greatest achievement was the lighting of the scene in which Rick Martin, reduced to dipsomania, staggers along W. 53rd Street past the honky-tonks and hot-spots to collapse next to a trash can in the gutter. McCord used neutral gray filters, which helped to create the effect of buildings casting deep shadows down an alley. Tilted cameras gave the impression of the character's drunkenness. It was a brilliantly effective sequence.

Perhaps the most famous *film noir* of the period was Howard Hawks' *The Big Sleep* (1946) adapted from Raymond Chandler's novel * by Leigh Brackett and William Faulkner. Chandler himself was pleased with the adaptation: he wrote to his British publisher, Hamish Hamilton, on May 30, 1946: "When and if you see the film of *The Big Sleep* (the first half of it anyhow) you will realize what can be done with this sort of story by a director with the gift of atmosphere and the requisite touch of hidden sadism." He also liked the casting of Bogart as Philip Marlowe, his jaded, bitter detective: "Bogart, of course, is so much better than any other tough-gut actor. As we say here, Bogie can be tough without a gun. Also he has a sense of humor that contains that grating undertone of contempt . . ."

Faulkner again provided convoluted dialogue which Leigh Brackett, experienced in the field of pulp fiction, managed to adapt into an idiomatic terseness; and he insisted upon working at his home in Missouri, which infuriated Jack Warner. But once again his approach to the construction of dramatic scenes was remarkably impressive.

Many of the scenes were improvised, added during shooting: Humphrey Bogart as Chandler's anti-hero Philip Marlowe was made to "camp" one scene, posing as a homosexual; a girl in a bookshop who seduces him was made to wear glasses, to give the sequence an unusual touch; and a sequence in which Bogart shot a man in cold blood was changed to one in which he forces him through a door, where he is mowed down by his own friends.† There was no logic or continuity in the story: once during the writing Hawks was forced to send a telegram to Ray-

---

* Published by Alfred Knopf in 1939. It was based on two sources: *Killer in the Rain*, a novelette published in 1935, and *The Curtain*, published in 1936.

---

† This stemmed from a suggestion made by the Breen office.

mond Chandler in New York asking the name of a killer; the reply came back immediately, but it made no sense. IMPOSSIBLE HE WAS AT THE BEACH AT THE TIME, Hawks cabled back. The film assumed the disconnected quality of a nightmare, staged in crowded sets based on close observation of Hollywood houses by Carl Jules Weyl, who devised much of the visual look of the picture, initially creating models with tiny figures in tiny sets.

John Huston made two *films noir* in the period: *Key Largo* and *The Treasure of the Sierra Madre.* The first of these was based on Maxwell Anderson's play about a group of people and a criminal gang isolated in a hotel in the Florida keys. It was a corruption of the already somewhat tired formula of Robert Sherwood's *The Petrified Forest,* to which it was quite uncomfortably similar in many details. Each of the characters was a grotesque stereotype: the fat gangster smoking a cigar in his bath (Edward G. Robinson), the bitter, jaded gang moll (Claire Trevor), the curmudgeonly, wheelchair-ridden hotelier (Lionel Barrymore). Bogart and Bacall re-created in a tired fashion their acidly affectionate maneuverings; the playing and writing, and the music of Max Steiner battling with a hurricane, all suggested that the formula of down-at-heel adventurers in an exotic setting was played out.

The Treasure of the Sierra Madre was as much of a corruption of *The Maltese Falcon* as *Key Largo* was of *The Petrified Forest.* Three men, in this version of a B. Traven novel, set out looking for gold in Mexico, and at the end they are faced with the hopelessness, the desolation of a life lived for greed.

The Treasure of the Sierra Madre was shot very largely in Mexico, in the area known as San Francisco, in Sanora and Tampico, and in San Jose di LaBrua, a hot springs resort. The last scene, in which the gold-seekers find that their gold dust is blowing away in a violent wind, was a major problem. The company propmen ran out of fuller's earth, which was usually used in combination with wind machines to send it whirling through the desert air, and even sway trees and tall cacti; they had to obtain two Air Force bombers from Mexico City, remove the wings, and turn on the engines to the highest available speed. The cement got into the eyes, the pores of the skin, and the lungs of director, actors and crew.

The *film noir* cycle brought about many technical improvements. In 1948 Warners released Transatlantic Pictures' *Rope*, directed by Alfred Hitchcock from the stage play based on the Leopold-Loeb case by Patrick Hamilton. Hitchcock originally discussed the idea in London in 1946, with the British theatre owner Sidney L. Bernstein. The intention was to shoot the action continuously, doing away entirely with the editing process, transferring the action from England to New York in the course of a few hours from late afternoon until late at night. Perry Ferguson, who had worked with Orson Welles on *Citizen Kane*, designed an effective set, done almost exactly to scale, of a penthouse fully furnished with living room, hall, and kitchen. On Sound Stage 12, working closely with Hitchcock, Ferguson added a new floor, raised four inches above the permanent one. It was completely lined in felt two inches thick. The walls were made of balsa wood and suspended from railings, removable or pushable so as to permit movement of the camera. Beyond the windows, which were of real glass in light aluminum frames, a model representing the New York skyline was arranged, accompanied by spun-glass clouds. The clouds were either suspended on wires or mounted on metal stands invisible to the naked eye catching the film. At the end of each reel, the workers on the set would change the clouds.

In many ways even more extraordinary as a photographic achievement, King Vidor's film *The Fountainhead* was a *film noir* based on a novel by Ayn Rand based on the career of Frank Lloyd Wright. In order to emphasize the ideals of the central figure, Howard Roark (Gary Cooper), who advocated an austere simplicity in his buildings, the style of the photography by Robert Burks had a bold cleanliness of line. Very little full light was used in the film, so as to insure a cold clarity of image. One important sequence was filmed in a granite quarry. Howard Roark, in order to experience the feeling of working on stone is stripped to the waist, the drill piercing the side of the cliff in an obvious symbol of his sexual virility as he is watched by an architecture critic, Dominique Franchon, played by Patricia Neal. The cameraman Robert Burks strove to give the scene the quality of a cubist painting, splitting the image into a succession of planes and hard blocks of black and white. In the rest of the film, the sets had been painted darker in the background by the art director, Edward Carrere, and lighter in the foreground, drenching them in a hard and intense light. In the quarry scene, shot at Knowles, California, Burks painted the face of the rock and filled actual shadows in with black embellishment. When the sun shifted its position, shadows were removed between shots and new patterns created.

In the last sequence of the film, Dominique Franchon ascends the tallest building in the world, the Winand Building, to meet Howard Roark. Herbert Lightman analyzed the sequence in the *American Cinematographer* (June, 1949): "[It required] a nightmare of special effects. Riding to the top of the elevator, she eventually reached a point where she is looking down on the Empire State Building. Glancing up she sees the rest of the building she is ascending, and to make this believable, the perspective (of the back projection) had to be changed constantly from floor to floor." Carrere designed more than 300 buildings for the film, including several working models.*

---

* Unfortunately, Jack Warner forbade King Vidor to engage Frank Lloyd Wright.

Bette Davis' vehicles had become less and less commercially acceptable in the period, and two films, *Winter Meeting,* in which she played a poet, and *Beyond the Forest,* in which she played an unhappy housewife in a travesty of *Mildred Pierce,* were commercial disasters. During an argument with King Vidor, the director of *Beyond the Forest,* Miss Davis announced that either Vidor would accept her decision in a scene in which she threw a bottle at a black maid, or she would quit. Vidor did not accept it, and she was released from her contract by Jack Warner.

Miss Davis' best film of the period was *A Stolen Life,* directed by Curtis Bernhardt for her own company and to an extent under her personal supervision. It was a new version of a film originally made with Elisabeth Bergner and Michael Redgrave in England in the 1930s. The story dealt with the then fashionable theme of twins, one of whom is good, one of whom is dissolute. The screenplay by Catherine Turney had great zest. A notable feature was the trick photography of Sol Polito. The problem was to show both Bette Davises in the same shot. Herbert Lightman discussed the handling of a scene in the *American Cinematographer* (June, 1946):

"To illustrate the general process used, let us take for example a scene from the picture in which Bette Davis is seated in a large chair. Her 'twin' crosses the screen and stands behind the chair talking to her. The scene was first shot with Miss Davis seated in the chair while a double went through the actions of the twin sister. Then another take was made of the same scene; this time with the double seated in the chair and Miss Davis taking the part of the other twin. In the special effects lab, the parts of both scenes which showed the double were masked out by means of irregular mattes, and the parts showing Miss Davis were then fitted together like an animated jig-saw puzzle, resulting in the illusion that she was playing opposite herself.

"In executing this effect the camera had to be securely clamped in place so that the backgrounds would match when the two fragments of the scene were printed together. Dialogue was keyed by means of a playback recording so that all of the action of both twins could be synchronized. The use of a double in parts of the scene to be masked out allowed her shadow to fall naturally about the set, and gave Miss Davis a chance to react normally to the dialogue and movements of another person. One scene called for a dolly shot of the twins walking down a long wharf. In the background crowds of people were milling about, crossing the set behind the two walking figures, and creating a good deal of background movement. This scene was shot in front of a process screen with Miss Davis on a treadmill to simulate the walking action. Separate takes were made of her on each side of the screen and the two were blended in the special effects lab. But because the background was moving, extreme care had to be taken to make sure that the background action on both halves would match. Here the blending had to be synchronized down to the last frame, and operation of the rear projector had to be absolutely consistent. A good deal of mathematics and timing entered into the process.

"In another scene Miss Davis lights a cigarette for her twin, smoothes her hair, etc. This was executed by having Miss Davis play the scene opposite a double who lit her cigarette and performed other actions at close range. Later, in the lab, just the double's face was masked out and Miss Davis' head was literally placed on her shoulders.

"Miss Davis screamed when she saw her headless body in a trial projection. 'Do they have to do that?' she cried as she started back from the image on the screen."

The finest sequence in this elaborate and handsome production was that in which a storm causes the drowning of one of the twins. As in *The Lighthouse by the Sea* some

20 years earlier, a special lighthouse was built at Laguna, and the scenes were matched in the studio tank. A yacht was floated in the tank, with wires which rocked it violently attached to the hull. Miss Davis was working with a stand-in while special dump tanks and a wind machine contrived to lash her violently. A sudden pitch of the vessel blew her into the water. Miss Davis went down to the bottom of the tank.

She became entangled in the wires and could not come up. She felt herself stifling. Fortunately, a special frogman was on hand to rescue her, or she would have been drowned.

In 1949, an odd development took place at the studio: following the sombre *films noirs* of the preceding four years, there was a sudden reversal to the mood of the early 1930s gangster films. The lighting was no longer lush and low-key; it was cold and harsh, the sets floodlit as they had been in the films of Alfred E. Green or Archie Mayo. The stories, no longer Germanic in their romantic fatalism, became once again sinewy accounts of crime, written without compromise. The whole new movement of the crime film was due, evidently, to the feeling of Jack Warner and Steve Trilling that Warners had too long been out of touch with the kind of picture it had made best. The result of this executive decision was a group of films that were among the finest the studio had ever produced, richer and more textured than the semi-documentary studies of crime being made simultaneously by the originator of the first cycle, Darryl F. Zanuck, at 20th Century-Fox.

In 1948, Virginia Kellogg, a gifted writer who had worked at Warners in the 1930s, had had a major success with her script for Anthony Mann's film *T-Men*, based on information supplied to her by treasury agents. Costing $400,000, the film had made four million. Milton Sperling, who was at the time married to Harry Warner's daughter Betty, and was a producer at Warners, summoned Miss Kellogg to his office and asked her to write a script which would rival *T-Men* as a commercial proposition. She set to work on a story, entitled *White Heat,* to be directed by Raoul Walsh. It was based once more on the activities of treasury men.

At first, she had intended combining the episode of Ma Barker and her gang in the 1930s with the story of a raid on the mint, and the theft of the contents of a mint truck in Denver, also in the 1930s. Unfortunately, Nellie Taylor-Ross, the head of the mint, forbade the idea; reluctantly, Miss Kellogg changed the narrative to include the theft of a railroad car. Her story followed Ma Barker and her psychotic son in a thinly disguised form through a series of murders and robberies until the gang's final arrest and destruction.

James Cagney, then making semi-independent films for release through Warners, liked the material, and felt that it would represent a return to the best qualities of *Public Enemy.* Unfortunately, Virginia Kellogg was working on a project at Universal and was unable to go ahead with a script, so Sperling engaged the team of Ivan Goff and Ben Roberts to proceed.

Cagney played Cody Jarrett, a murderous paranoid crook with an Oedipus complex, who, like the central character of Tom in *Public Enemy,* is played entirely without compromise. He is seized with violent attacks of pain (which he describes as "a red buzz-saw in my head"), shoots, kicks and maims without mercy. In the last scene, he is shown on top of an immense gas cylinder, with police surrounding him as he shouts, "Top of the world, ma!" and is blown to pieces. Cagney's performance was extraordinary: his bantam weight's stance, legs straddled wide, jaw jutting, cocky and arrogant, had never been better used. The frightening intensity of the playing reached a peak in a scene in San Quentin when he is seized by agonizing head pains, rushing through the crowd in the refectory with loud animal moans. Sid Hickox's photography, much of it in San Quentin itself, has an intense cold grayness, achieved in part by using as much actual daylight as possible.

Overlooked at the time, the succeeding Cagney vehicle, Gordon Douglas's *Kiss Tomorrow Goodbye*, was very nearly as good. Here, the attempt to re-create the formula of *Public Enemy* was really unmistakable: in one sequence, Cagney slapped his mistress, Barbara Payton, with a wet towel. Harry Brown's script, based on Horace McCoy's novel, showed Cagney as another paranoid hoodlum, Ralph Cotter, escaping from a prison farm, then performing a series of vicious crimes until he is murdered by his mistress. The story is framed in the trial of the murderess and her accomplices, the other members of the gang.

Brilliantly shot by Peverell Marley, the film was distinguished also by the firm and concentrated direction of Gordon Douglas, and by a marvelous portrait of corruption: the crooked attorney played to perfection by Luther Adler.

Inevitably, Warners revived the formula of *20,000 Years in Sing Sing* and made a film entitled *Caged* (1950), a story of a women's jail written admirably by Virginia Kellogg and directed by John Cromwell.

Jerry Wald, determined to retain his interest in films made for women, but still feeling the necessity to keep abreast of the new developments at the studio, had settled naturally on making a film about women's prisons. Copying an idea of Cecil B. DeMille's scenarist Jeanie Macpherson, who had once entered a jail in Michigan to research a story (*Manslaughter,* 1923), Wald sent Miss Kellogg into a series of corrective institutions. At first, she met with serious opposition. But she pointed out quite sharply that if she was refused permission to go to jail, she would make public the refusal. She would say that as a taxpayer she had been denied information about the prisons she helped to support. In consequence, she was admitted, provided she did not specifically name the jails in which she stayed.

In order to secure herself against suspicion, she invented a complicated story which did justice to her powers of invention. She said she was a bookkeeper who had helped her lover embezzle money in a war surplus arrangement. Her lover, she said, had left her in the lurch, forcing her to "face the music" in court. This tale, acted out in a suitably tough manner, earned the trust of her fellow prisoners. She managed to accumulate an ample dossier of material, showing the gross, corrupt prison matron, the bizarre inclinations of the criminals, the intolerable conditions of the "clinic" where babies were born.

In one prison, Miss Kellogg noted how a girl had her head shaved because she had attempted an escape or she had committed an act of lesbianism; in another, she saw prisoners beat spoons in anger on their metal dishes at a Christmas party because they had not received presents. She came to understand the agonized struggle for a woman to raise a baby or use lipstick, the evil matrons who used their privileges to obtain bribes; the gossip, laughter and misery of the "bullpens" or dormitories; the tension when a hated superintendent came by.

All of this information was poured into a remarkably detailed and intelligent script, and John Cromwell executed the film capably on floodlit sets by Charles H. Clarke, brutally photographed in grays and whites by Carl Guthrie. Eleanor Parker as the new inmate was based on two young girls Miss Kellogg met in jail; Agnes Moorehead played with sympathy the role of a prison superintendent; Hope Emerson played the hungry evil prison matron, munching caramels and humming triumphantly after ordering each new torture.

Miss Emerson's performance was indeed so realistic

that when she wheeled her crippled mother through the lobby after the Los Angeles premiere, she was hissed by the crowd; her death on the screen was greeted with an extraordinary outbreak of cheers and applause.

After reviving the prison film, Jerry Wald revived the story of the activities of the Ku Klux Klan in the Deep South, reverting to the theme of *Black Legion.* Daniel Fuchs and Richard Brooks wrote for him the script of *Storm Warning* (1951); the director was Stuart Heisler, distinguished for his excellent films *The Biscuit Eater* and *Crack-Up.* The opening sequence of *Storm Warning*—photographed with deliberate crudity by Carl Guthrie—was brilliantly done. A woman, played by Ginger Rogers, arrives in a sleepy small town by bus. Stepping out, she is the witness to a murder by the Klan. The sweaty streets, the screech of the bus' wheels, the white hoods against the intense darkness, a single terrified face disclosed in a torch beam: Heisler's mastery of the *mise en scène* rivals that of Mervyn Le Roy in *They Won't Forget.* And later, as the newcomer discovers that the killer whose face she has seen is her own brother-in-law, the tension is drawn very tight.

Steve Cochran gave a remarkable performance of the cowardly, degenerate employee of the Klan, virile and swaggering on the outside, defeated and miserable within. Another impressive addition to the series of films was Bretaigne Windust's *The Enforcer,* based by Martin Rackin on an original story by the same John Bright who had come to Hollywood more than 20 years before to write *Public Enemy.* Here, Humphrey Bogart played a crusading district attorney who breaks up a crime ring, Murder Incorporated. The photography of Robert Burks was grimly accurate, the direction intense and powerful. This group of films enormously enhanced the post-war reputation of the studio.

14

Years of
Decline

T HE CYCLE OF FILMS
dealing with social themes ran out in 1952, and firmly
marked the end of Warner Brothers as a vital and independent organ of opinion. It was obviously only a question of time before, in the wake of the blacklist and in
common with most other Hollywood studios, Warners became intellectually bankrupt, unable to purvey radical
ideas lest they should be thought to be indicative of sub-
version.

The early 1950s were years of serious distress at the
studio. The deaths of Carl Jules Weyl in 1948 and of Joseph Valentine in 1949 were grievous blows. Harry and
Jack Warner quarreled constantly. Jerry Wald became irri-
tated about the number of his properties which were rejected by Steve Trilling and Jack Warner. On June 17,

1951, he accepted an offer from Howard Hughes, then the managing director of RKO-Radio Pictures, who bought his contract for $150,000. Wald had been with the studio for 19 years. Almost on that same day, Warners concluded its arrangements with the government for the severance of its theatre interests. Two separate companies would be formed without mutual officers or directors. Officers or directors with more than one percent of stock must sell that stock in either one company or the other within twelve months.

By the outset of 1951, the company's net profits had sunk from $22,094,979 in 1947 to $9,427,344. Jack Warner and Steve Trilling arranged * for the dismissal of more than 25 percent of the publicity staff in addition to those men in charge of labor relations, work orders, and time keeping. All three of these were taken in charge by Edmund L. DePatie, the studio business manager. On April 29, the head of the special effects department and the story editor were fired. On May 3, the brothers issued a despairing statement: "We will sell out and retire if somebody makes the right offer."

By this stage, their position had grown so grievous that they had disposed of all except 24 percent of Warner stock, 18 percent of it owned by themselves, and 6 through relatives. A real estate man in San Francisco, Louis R. Lurie, offered 25 million dollars for the family interest. Harry Warner told *The New York Times:* "If he has the money $25 million is an agreeable price. The chances are we can make a deal. Actually there has been nothing but a lot of talk yet, but we are interested in disposing of our stock if the right fellow comes across."

It emerged that Lurie represented a syndicate which included the Transamerica Corporation. On May 5 he was

---

* Trilling himself was subsequently dismissed by Warner without warning.

joined by the Hollywood producer Sol Lesser, who sought to purchase a substantial portion of the company. Other members of the Syndicate were listed by *The New York Times* on May 8: Clinton Murchison, the Dallas banker and insurance executive; Arde Bulova, Board Chairman of the Bulova Watch Company; Lee Shubert, the theatrical leader; Nat Cummings, of Consolidated Grovers' Corporation of Chicago and various New York brokers.

The meetings on the sale broke down rapidly. Harry Warner became sickened by the discussions over the value of the great company he had helped to found. For the time being, he told *The New York Times*, he would continue in business, but only a few weeks later he was talking to Serge Semenenko, the Boston banker, about a sale.

During these unhappy years of change Jack Warner made bold efforts to combat the public's flagging interest in motion pictures. Alongside the series of crime films, he made a succession of gaudy musicals similar to those which Darryl F. Zanuck had fostered at 20th Century-Fox.

The colors of these films were bright and cheerful, the pace fast and snappy. But these films were a far cry from the backstage stories of the early 1930s. They were somewhat mindless and over-sweet, with the exception of an agreeably acid version of *Life with Father*, starring William Powell, directed with flair by Curtiz, and a nimble remake of *Charley's Aunt, Where's Charley?* attractively directed on English locations by David Butler, and starring a genius among American dancers, the angularly witty Ray Bolger.

The most famous of the musicals of the period were those starring Doris Day. Reminiscent of the late Marilyn Miller in her tough, sunny extroversion, she first appeared in a folderol called *Romance on the High Seas*, directed by Curtiz. Thereafter she made a succession of films, including *My Dream Is Yours* and *Calamity Jane*, which made her the most successful female star in America during the saccharine 1950s.

The action film returned as the main source of financial returns and, as in 1923, the studio began to make films in the actual West. Alongside the musicals—which included a remake of *The Jazz Singer* and yet another *Desert Song*, such films as *The Man behind the Gun, The Charge at Feather River, Plunder of the Sun, Island of the Sky, The Diamond Queen, Thunder over the Plains, The Moonlighter, Blowing Wild* and a remake of *So Big* had much of the skill, if little of the energy which had characterized the studio's silent films of the out-of-doors. None is worthy of remembrance. Alongside these features, the studio continued to make its famous series of *Joe McDoakes* comedies, its sports parodies, *Vitaphone Varieties, Bugs Bunny* cartoons, *Merrie Melodies and Loony Tunes*, its *Blue Ribbon Hit Parades* and *Melody Master Tunes*.

In something of a desperate move, Jack Warner became interested in three-dimensional movies during 1952. He had seen a very bad film entitled *Bwana Devil*, directed by Arch Oboler, made in 3-D in 1952. It had been financed by an enthusiastic promoter, Milton Gunzburg, who had based his concept on a device put together by a cameraman, Friend Baker. Warner called Gunzburg after a successful opening in Los Angeles and offered him the chance to make two productions in the system. He decided upon remaking *The Mystery of the Wax Museum*, directed by Michael Curtiz in 1933. Oddly, he elected as the director of *House of Wax* a man, Andre deToth, who had only one eye. Mr. deToth was therefore the only director in Hollywood who could not see in three dimensions.

Crane Wilbur's screenplay removed the black comedy from the original film, which had largely been embodied in the character of a typical girl reporter. He set the action back more effectively in the late 19th century, in a carefully suggested theatrical milieu. But unfortunately the direction, and the design of Stanley Fleischer, quite lacked the brilliance of the work of Curtiz and Anton Grot in the original film. The novelty proved commercially viable, but the film was poorly reviewed and offered no help to the prestige of the studio. The vogue was short-lived and Warners made little else in the genre.

In the mid-1950s the company gradually but definitely began to fall apart. On April 9, 1953, executives took pay cuts of up to 50 percent. The studio closed down for 90 days. On July 15, Max Steiner left the studio after 16 years, just after completing *The Boy from Oklahoma,* which also marked the end of Michael Curtiz' long reign as the most important director of the studio. A rather feeble attempt was made to combat CinemaScope, which had now been introduced by the efforts of Spyros Skouras at 20th Century-Fox and had reactivated that company. Jack Warner attempted by making a deal with Zeiss-Optikon in Germany to obtain lenses for "Warner Super Scope" different from those used for CinemaScope. But by October 23 the system had proved unsatisfactory at prior tests and the studio entered into an agreement with 20th Century-Fox. Albert Warner issued a pious statement: "We believe that the industry can best be served by leading producers collaborating and cooperating on technical advances for the best interests of the business."

On May 17, 1952, a major fire broke out in the studio. Sound stage 21 collapsed and a set being used for the film *The Iron Mistress* was destroyed. Executives helped to fight the fire with hoses, and it was rapidly extinguished. But on July 10 a much worse conflagration broke out, at 3 o'clock in the afternoon. It began, apparently, at the boat dock at the southern extremity of the Burbank back-lot; the property shed, containing an invaluable amount of props going back to the Lubitsch and Rin-Tin-Tin films, was destroyed. A 1200-foot scene dock, electronic equipment valued at $500,000 and various sets were ruined. The production of yet another version of *The Desert Song* was brought to a halt, and the *Stop, You're Killing Me* company helped to fight the fire. The police arson squad chief Sergeant Ed Hatcher believed that the fire had been deliberately started, but he was unable to prove anything.

An important addition to the studio in its dark days of decline was a remarkable young actor, James Dean. Nervous, intense, vulnerable, he had a touch of genius not recognized at the time. Dean's biggest success was in Billy Rose's production of Andre Gide's *The Immoralist*, with Geraldine Page and Louis Jourdan. His performance, under the direction of Daniel Mann, won him the David Blum Award. When Dean's agent Jane Deacy happened upon Paul Osborn's screenplay based on Steinbeck's *East of Eden*, she at once insisted on Dean trying out for the part of the sensitive and nervous youth Cal Trask. Jack Warner was uneasy about casting Dean, but Hedda Hopper was fascinated when Dean visited her at her house on Tropical Avenue, and she used her influence on his behalf. Elia Kazan was deeply impressed by Dean's test and engaged him at once.

Osborn's script was based on the last quarter of John Steinbeck's novel. Adam Trask has found a home in the lettuce country near Salinas in northern California with his two sons Cal and Aron. The script centers on the character of Cal: his withdrawn, awkward, compulsive spirit is torn by jealousy of his brother, played by Richard Davalos, and a deep hatred of his mother, the town madam, played with a shrewd intelligence by Jo Van Fleet. Abra, exquisitely acted by the young and hauntingly beautiful Julie Harris, is the girl with whom Adam is obsessed.

The biblical parallels may have been rather strained, and Kazan's direction excessively mannered, but the beautifully sustained script was a pleasure. And Ted Mc-Cord's subdued, almost monochrome photography, the color deliberately desaturated, had all of the nostalgic charm of an album of 1917, the year in which the story was set.

The art direction of James Basevi and Malcolm Bert was miraculously right, and the score of Leonard Rosenman had a subtle period charm quite unlike the more highly powered excesses of Max Steiner.

The reviews of James Dean's performance were not warm, but he had become an immediate and extraordinary hit with the public. In an age when youth—or the movie image of youth—was cleansed and standardized, he represented a figure convincingly sullen, agonized, withdrawn. Better than anyone else, he represented the fact that youth was seldom the happiest season. He was so vulnerable he seemed to be a man without a skin: audiences instinctively responded to his suggested bisexuality, his odd combination of masculine virility and feminine softness and insecurity. Dean's halting Strasberg Method delivery did not interfere with the spontaneous warmth and freedom of his playing. As he danced over a field, freshly sprouting the new bean crop, he was the epitome of youth. It was an un-self-conscious moment in an otherwise vividly self-conscious performance. It was unfortunate that Kazan's direction, deliberate and theatrical in its emphases, somewhat eliminated the sense of tenderness and youthful wonder that the material called for. But the film was important, nonetheless.

East of Eden proved that, in the early days of wide screen, Warners had not lost its concern with social themes. Heavily symbolic and over-wrought though it was, *East of Eden* was a pioneer work in showing the widening rift of the American generations. Though set almost 40 years before the time in which it was made, it was wholly contemporary in its orientation.

Immediately afterward, Jack Warner arranged for Dean to appear in Stewart Stern's *Rebel without a Cause,* which became virtually a seminal work of its period. It portrayed a calm, middle-class suburban world within which the tensions between the generations are violently extreme. Jim Backus is Dad, a feeble, witless and self-defeating weakling who has surrendered his manhood. Mother, as played by Ann Doran, is frustrated and desperate. Natalie Wood, the delicate neighbor girl, is sensitive and misunderstood. The stereotypes are crudely drawn. But the execution by Nicholas Ray, the director, is accomplished, and his response to the problems of youth deeply sympathetic. The hot nights and profound sexual hungers of a suburban milieu are expertly and thoughtfully realized; in one sequence, the Chicken Run episode in which youths compete with each other in dilapidated jalopies in a drag race, Ray brilliantly hit off the essence of a period and a style. A switchblade fight is handled with a tense effectiveness, and the wide screen is marvelously used at the climax: a gunfight is staged against the severe planes and curves of the Hayden Planetarium.

Dean's controlled fierceness in the film was far removed from the deliberate indifference and "cool" of the 1970s. Once again, he was not uniformly well treated by critics, and once again that did not matter. Even before *Rebel without a Cause* was finished, he decided to obtain the most important role of all: that of Jett Rink in George Stevens' *Giant,* based on the novel of Edna Ferber by Fred Guiol and Ivan Moffat.

The story was excessively diffuse. A Texas rancher, Bick Benedict (Rock Hudson) meets a lovely girl, Leslie Lynton (Elizabeth Taylor) in Maryland while buying horses. At the family estate, Leslie is involved in numerous quarrels with Luz Benedict, Bick's repressed, probably incestuous sister, who is killed while out riding. Jett Rink (Dean) is a ranch hand who suddenly strikes oil on his small piece of territory. The bulk of the film deals with the complex relationships of Bick, Leslie and Jett.

The film is an uneven, sometimes halting chronicle. But there are passages in it as magnificent as any that came out of the Warner studio, in which Stevens' direction surmounts the irritating fluctuations of the wide-screen color system.

As in many of his films, Stevens believed in shooting at times of day generally considered unsuitable for color photography: late afternoon just before sunset, or very early in the morning. He used a total of 20,000 setups, shooting scenes from every conceivable angle, "covering" himself in a manner which no earlier Warner director would have tolerated. When his thoughtful, laborious style worked, it worked very effectively. In the scene in which Mercedes McCambridge's Luz Benedict is killed in a fall from her horse, Stevens and his cameraman William C. Mellor took the shot from an immense distance. Without warning, Stevens cut to a close-up of her boot, sharply spurred, urging the horse along. In one remarkable moment, the scene conveyed the space, distance and dust of the environment, the anguish of the frustrated spinster, the thrust of the spurs which indicated the knife stab of sexual frustration, and the precise cause of her death. The shots of the riderless horse pounding against a raw blue sky were strikingly poetic, superior to anything in the prose of the novel. Other scenes are almost as fine: the sudden gush of oil which promises wealth and freedom to Jett Rink is a symbol of the American dream of power and money swiftly and miraculously achieved. In this great Warner film, as Jett Rink splashed in the oil, ecstatically crying out, his body saturated in black liquid, we see an image of American triumph and decay caught in the same unforgettable moment.

James Dean's death in a car crash after the conclusion of his role in *Giant* was symbolic of the crushed hopes of the Warners themselves. Only two years later Jack Warner himself almost died in a similar crash in the south of France. Harry Warner died in 1958. But in the meantime, they had succeeded in providing an unforgettable monument, a symbol of the studio's collective genius, and a masterpiece of the modern film: *A Star Is Born.*

15

A Star
Is Born

EACH OF THE MAJOR
Hollywood studios had worked towards one great film,
one masterpiece which would sum up all of its skills in a
single tremendous effort of talent and will. At Columbia,
that film had been *Lost Horizon* in the 1930s; at Selznick,
Gone with the Wind; at M-G-M, *The Good Earth* and *The
Wizard of Oz;* at Paramount, *The Lady Eve;* at 20th Century-Fox, *In Old Chicago* and *The Rains Came.* Warners
was the last to make a rich demonstration of its genius.
That film was *A Star Is Born,* made in 1954, and it was not
subsequently equalled by any other studio as a study of
show business from the inside. It contained the finest performance of James Mason; it contained George Cukor's
greatest direction and Moss Hart's best dialogue; the musical direction of Ray Heindorf was the best work he ever

did at the studio; the songs of Harold Arlen and Ira Gershwin were inspired; and Sam Leavitt's photography was the most skilled, the most dynamic ever seen in the ratio of CinemaScope.

A *Star Is Born* was above all the most important vehicle for the talents of Judy Garland, an actress of transcendent technique, open vulnerability and daring, and a profound sense of the true emotion in a scene. The film was hers from beginning to end, and she never equalled it. Its creation followed a period of severe distress in Judy Garland's life. She had been dismissed by M-G-M, which had developed her career from childhood. She had attempted to cut the arteries in her wrists, and had divorced her husband, the director Vincente Minnelli.

A number of stage appearances had partly restored her confidence, and her second husband, a former agent named Sid Luft, also helped to reconstruct her shattered ego. He persuaded her to undertake a new screen appearance. In early discussions, they agreed upon remaking A *Star Is Born*, the story of a rising actress and the falling star she marries. Together, the Lufts spoke with the producer Edward L. Alperson, who had acquired the rights, and formed a company, Transcona (a condensation of Transcontinental America) with Miss Garland as a member of the board of directors. Alperson made an arrangement with Warners, and a budget was fixed: initially $1.8 million. Moss Hart was engaged to write the script; according to an article in *Time* magazine, he requested the sum of $100,000, a house in Palm Springs, and a beach house at Malibu in payment for his efforts; James Mason received $125,000 for 12 weeks' work and $12,500 for all subsequent weeks.

The origins of A *Star Is Born* were complex. Adela Rogers St. Johns had written the original story, based on an actual episode of the 1920s in which she witnessed an alcoholic male star, John Bowers, swim to his death in the

Pacific Ocean. She had actually been present in his beach house when the tragedy occurred. Her story, *What Price Hollywood?* was filmed by George Cukor in 1932, produced by David O. Selznick, with Constance Bennett and Lowell Sherman in the leading roles. Cool and frank, it had many sharp and witty episodes, but did not quite work as a whole. In 1937 Selznick decided to make the story again, with Fredric March and Janet Gaynor. Unfortunately, Cukor was not available to direct. The film was directed by William Wellman and written by Robert Cerson and Alan Campbell and Campbell's wife, Dorothy Parker. It was crudely put together, but hit off with a degree of sharpness the Hollywood environment; Janet Gaynor's desperate earnestness was appropriate to the character of Esther Blodgett, the pathetic out-of-towner who becomes a major Hollywood star.

Esther Blodgett is singing in a small downtown Hollywood nightclub when she is spotted by a restless and promiscuous star, Norman Maine. He picks her up, they enter an affair, and he has her screen-tested. She is a great success and is signed to a long-term contract. But Maine is an alcoholic and he gradually sinks as she rises; once his box-office significance is over, he commits suicide; with considerable effort of will, Esther Blodgett—now renamed Vicki Lester—decides to continue with her career.

The story is merely serviceable, and in other hands it could have been a soap opera. But Hart's script superbly uses the slender premise as a means of exposing the realities of Hollywood. The weakness and narcissism, the insecurity and passionate concentration of the star personality have never been so painstakingly and accurately observed. Norman Maine, on the surface a smooth sophisticate, at heart a childish weakling, is given all of the charm and softness that the character calls for. Vicki Lester is equally well drawn: her vibrant, electric attack and style contrasted with her deep sense of fear, anxiety and defeat. The press agent, ready to kick the big-timer when he is down; the mercurial studio chief; the pitiless fans and hangers-on: these are observed with a piercing scrutiny by the writer. If anything, the script is more savagely critical of the public than it is of the industry itself. The mob of star-followers is shown as animalistic and mindless, at once sycophantic and deadly.

George Cukor was the ideal director for the task. When Sid Luft invited him to lunch at Romanoffs and began to say that he had a subject for Judy Garland, Cukor stopped him before he announced what it was and said, "If it's for her I'll do it, no matter what it is." The deal was made on a handshake. Cukor had only worked with her once before: making tests for *The Wizard of Oz*. But he had always deeply admired her and she had adored his work. A sophisticated, amusing, vastly intelligent man, with a fine record of direction which included Greta Garbo's *Camille* and a version of Clare Booth Luce's *The Women*, he knew Hollywood intimately, with a combination of affection and wry analysis. His precisely correct evocation of the milieu was as much a pleasure as Moss Hart's faithfully observant scenario.

An important question was to select the composer and lyricist: Ira Gershwin and Harold Arlen were brilliantly "right" choices. As the actor who would play the leading male role, Humphrey Bogart and Frank Sinatra were mentioned. Tremendous efforts were made to secure Cary Grant for the role. George Cukor, in particular, felt that he would be absolutely ideal. Grant insisted upon reading for it, which he did with a halting, insecure but deeply moving effect. Cukor was very excited, but unfortunately at the very last minute negotiations for Grant fell through, and he withdrew. Instead, Jack Warner, Cukor, Garland and Luft all decided upon James Mason. He was available and had a marvelous selfless patience which made him the perfect star to work with.

Mason was the perfect foil for Judy Garland. Quite obviously a more extrovert player—someone of the character of Sinatra for instance—would have been too strong, not only taking away from Miss Garland, but also providing too little contrast with her brilliantly exaggerated, openly emotional and vibrant, electric playing. James Mason, an "interior" actor with deep reserves of feeling, everything withdrawn, hidden and conserved behind a bland, slightly soft "front," was ideally placed in the material. The effect of his breakdown would be all the more effective for the restraining of emotion which had preceded it: the moment at the end when Norman Maine breaks down because he knows that all he can do is to die would be doubly heartrending.

A Star Is Born was begun on October 12, in Warner SuperScope, but after the brilliantly successful premiere of *The Robe,* the first film in CinemaScope, Jack Warner was compelled to bow the knee to 20th Century-Fox and make the film in CinemaScope. Happily, however, the studio used the Technicolor laboratories for the processing instead of the DeLuxe laboratories, which were making weak and poorly colored prints of the Fox films. The cameraman Milton Krasner began making tests in mid-October, 1953, based on his experience at Fox, beginning with a run-through of the famous Harold Arlen song "Lose That Long Face." All of the original footage was scrapped—fortunately, due to an illness of James Mason, not a great deal had been shot by Winton Hoch—and the whole picture started again under the director of photography, Sam Leavitt, whom Miss Garland requested. He had been her camera operator at M-G-M.

Leavitt was a master of mood. In the scenes in which Judy Garland is happy, a very high key was used; as she gradually sank into unhappiness, and lost her husband, the mood grew more somber, until, in a sequence after his death in which she sat brooding in a firelit room, the screen was almost dark.

One famous scene showed Garland singing Harold Arlen's "The Man That Got Away" in a small nightclub; she is discovered there by James Mason. Cukor wanted the faces of the band blacked out so that all that could be seen was the gleaming outlines of the instruments and Judy Garland's own face emerging from the darkness. Leavitt raised the incandescent lights so that the performer's faces were not automatically illuminated, while at the same time he illuminated Miss Garland's own. He blocked off large areas of the screen in heavy shadows. The general theory at the time was that in CinemaScope a high degree of candlepower from 400 up had to be used so that the delicate stock could properly be developed. Both Cukor and Leavitt decided to ignore these restrictions, and a great deal of the film was lit in a manner not highly thought of at the time. The results were exceptionally beautiful.

It was the first scene to be shot. Jack Warner was deeply impressed by it, and insisted on shaking Leavitt's hand.

Another extraordinary sequence took place at the Shrine Auditorium, at a first night in which Judy Garland appears in a stage show, and James Mason joins drunkenly in the chorus line. The introductory shot shows the camera photographing an enormous open arc light—a staggering feat, especially since the lens showed hardly any reflections. Leavitt and his crew were on a 40-foot crane and shot down on the crowd, an effect which was later expertly matched to the shots of the crowd at the premiere of *The Robe*. Inside the Auditorium itself, Leavitt's wizardry made 600 people look like 6000—again by blocking out areas in shadow, and using a dazzle of cross lighting. On the stage, several cameras with a multiplicity of setups were expertly deployed, again with direct shooting on this occasion into whole banks of multicolored lights. The whole Auditorium had to be completely relit from top to bottom, a whole range of arcs specially graduated with filters and dimmers as they stretched in line into the darkest recesses of the stage. Beams slanted across the image, refracted over and over again.

Judy Garland herself was illuminated by a moving spotlight. Since an actual spotlight from behind the balcony would diffuse her figure rather than give precisely the correct intensity of light, Leavitt set up a "hot" spotlight right under the balcony, giving a smaller "throw." A sequence at a beach house in which James Mason swims to his death was wonderfully managed. First, Leavitt shot Mason running into the sea against the setting sun, a sequence which George Cukor directed over and over again to get precisely the right "dying fall" feeling of a light, and a life, fading. Then in the studio the set of the beach house was photographed with the ocean as a back projection. A wind tunnel tossed long curtains, to give an effect of ocean breeze, and the back projection reflected in the glass, with Judy Garland moving against the reflection casting very oblique shadows.

George Cukor worked very closely with the Russian color consultant George Hoyningen-Huene, and the skillful designer Gene Allen. These gifted and expansive men were of great help in preparing the production. In conference in Cukor's office, they fully discussed scenes; on the set, Huene and Allen provided richly suggestive ideas for Cukor and Sam Leavitt to work on. Their main problem was to solve the difficulty of wide screen. They noticed that Henry King, in directing *The Robe*, had made the cast stand in straight lines. They worked out how to dispose the figures in depth. Studying the work of Tou-

215

louse-Lautrec, they determined that he divided some of his compositions with thin poles or other vertical divisions, so they used a variety of objects to split the frame. With no ceiling or floor lines, just a letterbox slit across the image, the team had a problem of suggesting dimension. They used table tops, or fake ceilings, to break up the line of vision, often striking out boldly against the very shape of the screen itself. The technical advisers ruled their efforts as futile, but they proceeded with brilliant success. As an example of their combined skills, the funeral scene following the death of Norman Maine may be cited. It was raining when the unit began work at the Church of the Good Samaritan, and the view of several people at the studio was that therefore the scene could not be shot, but the team worked out that a rainy effect would be striking: a thunderous sky, faces under umbrellas, umbrellas black and menacing and spined like bats' wings moving in, the crowd thrusting forward hysterically and greedily as Vicki Lester leaves the church, a scene of transcendent horror climaxed with a shot of a woman ripping off her veil, predatory cries, and a close-up of the star's face, her mouth opening in a scream of terror.

Another remarkable scene was set in an alcoholic home in which Norman Maine is incarcerated following a monumental binge. Gene Allen reworked an existing set which had been used in various forms since the 1940s. George Cukor had visited John Barrymore in a similar place, and effectively reconstructed it from his memory: the brown and pallid green walls and curtains, the drab beige blind, the windows furred with dust, the seedy sunporch where the sick man sat. Sam Leavitt's lighting had a subdued and somber quality entirely in keeping with the scene. Gene Allen had been born in a similar environment, and supplied many ideas, including the high surface polish on the wood to "improve" its appearance, and the bevelled glass windows which looked at once elaborate and redolent of poverty, what Allen called "that Pasadena look."

During the shooting, Judy Garland was frequently late on the set, and the budget rose horrifically. Cukor often had to go into her dressing room and plead with her to proceed with a scene. The reason for her dilatoriness was not a form of perversity, but rather a need to make sure that whenever she was called for, she was absolutely "right." She refused to play when she was not completely in command. The result was that every scene she played was astonishing in its accuracy, that there were no slack moments; and it is very much to Jack Warner's credit that he stood by her, endured all the delays, and did not interfere with her at all. Cukor never ceased to marvel at the poignancy and sincerity of her playing. Her finest scene was when, following the death of her husband, she is persuaded to go to a premiere. Cukor told her to "go off the deep end," to be totally depressed, to risk ugliness by releasing the emotion completely. She simply let fly, stumbling over her words, struggling to speak; and Cukor, watching her, felt goose pimples: the certain instinct that he was looking at a supremely great actress. She was angry, bitter, she cried; and when the actor Tommy Noonan stood between her and her desire to cling to her loneliness of grief, she struggled with him in a hideous, almost unbearably "real" way. Finally, terrified that there might be something wrong with the film, Cukor took his courage in both hands and asked her to play the scene again. Typically, she said: "Come around to my house any afternoon, and you'll see me playing that scene." Then she paused. "But not twice. Not twice."

She played it a second time quite perfectly, and the results were brilliantly effective.

The premiere of *A Star Is Born* was the last great event in the history of Warner Brothers. On the night of September 29, 1954, a crowd of 20,000 filled the streets outside the Pantages Theatre on Hollywood Boulevard. Marlene Dietrich arrived in an open limousine, with Elia Kazan as her escort. Judy Garland's voice delivered the Arlen/Gershwin songs over a dozen loudspeakers. Searchlights ranged across the sky. Jack Carson and George Jessel compered the arrival of the stars in the lobby. The Gary Coopers, Edward G. Robinson, Michael Wilding and his wife Elizabeth Taylor, Kim Novak, Ann Miller, Joan Crawford, Rock Hudson: it was the most extraordinary collection of figures to have attended a similar event since the 1920s. Judy Garland herself was greeted with an obligatory barrage of screams.

As the audience settled in its seats, there was a sense of excitement comparable only with that which greeted the opening of *The Jazz Singer* almost 30 years before. It was almost as though every single person present knew that this was to be a tremendous production, a testimonial to the skills not only of its director and players but to the superb showmanship of Jack Warner himself, that it would not be equalled by the studio. What no one could have known was that it would also be the last of the great "Hollywood studio" pictures, a summation of the very character of the environment. The curtains parted, the orchestra under Ray Heindorf excitingly struck up the theme of "The Man That Got Away," the credits in bold and splashy red flared out against a glittering skyline of Los Angeles. *A Star Is Born* began. . . .

Index

Index

Index